T0113930

Finding Your Niche & Maintaining Your Pastoral Poise

THOUGHTS
FOR
THE
NEW PASTOR

FOR THE FIRST YEARS IN PASTORAL MINISTRY

REV. RK SHORTER

authorHOUSE®

AuthorHouse™
1663 Liberty Drive
Bloomington, IN 47403
www.authorhouse.com
Phone: 833-262-8899

Published by AuthorHouse 12/21/2020

ISBN: 978-1-6655-1147-6 (sc)
ISBN: 978-1-6655-1168-1 (e)

Library of Congress Control Number: 2020925364

Print information available on the last page.

Credits to Michael A. Sizemore, Mountain Artworks Studio Athens, WV for the cover image use in the book.

This book is printed on acid-free paper.

Regarding Rev. Robby Shorter's book
Finding Your Niche & Maintaining Your Pastoral Poise:

While reading this book, I was able to recall and relate to events that were shared, from being called to the ministry, to answering that call. Chapter Four was a special chapter that spoke to me as it pertained to changing perspectives and churches. Each chapter is a glimpse of things to come, maybe not in exactly the same way, but in some similar form. As I read this work, I realized that I would have loved to have had this book when I began ministry those many years ago. I honestly believe God has led the telling of each chapter of this book and it would prove to be a great help for anyone that is about to go forward in ministry as it covers a many areas in which we have all found ourselves going through.

When I first met Robby, I knew there was something about him and I knew God had a calling for him. I am so happy that Reverend Shorter has followed the call of God and has now reached out with this book to help others starting their ministry journey. May God continue to bless my brother, and may God bless those who read this book.

I hereby given my permission to use this in this wonderful book.

Earl Pennington, Elder
WV South District, Church of the Nazarene

Contents

Acknowledgements

I want to give special thanks to my wife Debra, and acknowledge her for being such a strong partner in our ministry.

Thank you, Pastor Gerald and Annette Kincaid, for being there for us and listening from your heart as I was trying to explain my hearts feelings to you in those first days of our friendship. I thank God that you listened and were willing to support and encourage our efforts as we began our first steps toward Pastoral Ministry. As you have now stepped back from ministry and re-retired, you can do so knowing that your work continues in us.

Pastor Erma Jean Hudgins, Thank you for giving a very young minister the opportunity to preach those very first sermons. You provided some wonderful wisdom that has proven very helpful, and subsequently, many families. Just think, it only took twenty-five years for me to get it together.

Rev. Earl Pennington, Thank you for always being that spiritual brother with a big shoulder, and a voice of concern and reason. Thank you for being a voice of reality, and always being ready to help and support us in every way possible. Your efforts and counsel will always be valued and welcomed.

Rev. John Vance, Ph.D. Thank you for the privilege of your friendship. Thank you for proofing this writing and sharing your support, your wisdom, and your expertise.

I want to give thanks to the churches that Deb and I have been honored to serve in our ministry. Thank you for your love and support that has been shown to us during those first important days, weeks, and years of ministry. Thank you for the patience and contributions made to our lives.

Just as I received help and encouragement, I now wish to offer it to those taking the next steps.

God bless you and keep you as you declare Jesus to the world.

Preface

This book is directed to those shiny eyes and big soft hearts that have answered the call to ministry, or, are still trying to discern their call to ministry. I wrote this book with one purpose and it was to offer help to those that are starting their first steps in pastoral ministry. The first weeks, months, and years are very special but can seem quite scary.

Each journey and experience in pastoral ministry is different; however, there are many similarities that we all will face along the way, as will those coming along after us. I know that I encountered experiences in my first years that I could have surely appreciated a "*time out*" conversation from someone wiser and more experienced than I.

It is hoped that you will read this material and retain something that will be a positive asset as you begin your early steps in ministry. I pray it will be of use in a way that will help you on your way to a fulfilling spiritual journey in the service of Jesus Christ. The lifelong call into serving Christ in a pastoral ministry can be very challenging and we need all the help we can get. This book equates to a "*Pastoral Primer*" and it might also serve as a good read for churches in search of a pastor. It could provide a better understanding to church members and committees of what it feels like to walk in a pastors shoes and carry their load.

We all need encouragement and advice! This is a journey that will give you a view from the highest mountains one moment and greatly challenge your patience the next. You may not love every minute of it, but, you will come to realize that serving Christ is an honor and a privilege. It is worth it!

*Some were called. Some were sent. Some
just picked up the book and went*!

Author unknown.

Foreword

If you are holding this book and reading these words, WELCOME! If you have found yourself inexplicably interested and attracted to my book about pastoral ministry, Praise the Lord! I do not believe in mere coincidences. If you are trying to decide if you really want to go further and purchase this book, let me ask you a question before you spend the money. What is your goal? Are you reading this to gain a deeper doctrinal and theological understanding of ministry? Are you looking for case studies that were performed in an inner-city, or underserved area in a major metropolitan area? If your answer is yes, *please do not buy this book*. If someone got you this book as a gift, knowing that you enjoy being involved in this particular style of reading, *this will probably not be the book for you!*

I suspect you will not enjoy the book if these are your reading interests. BUT, if you are looking for a simple read, one that speaks from the heart, and speaks about what those first weeks, months, and years might look like as a pastor, this **might just be the book for you!** Are you excited? I have encountered many books during my pastoral studies that were written on a level way above my head. Sadly, I learned very little from those authors, and if it had not been for wisdom and the grace of the course instructors, I might have gone away from some of those classes disappointed. I required something that I was able to sit down and read, something I could sink my teeth into, something I was able to relate to and comprehend and something I could apply to my own ministry situation. I know that I am not alone in this area and felt driven and inspired to write something others could easily understand and follow. I aspire to write something that I thought I might have benefited from reading early on in my career. I have great respect for those educated writers, and also for their wonderful contributions to our field. My learning style required something different to allow me the ability to grasp and apply to my situation. Maybe, this relates to your situation too? It is possible.

The targeted readers of this book are those people new in ministry, or those that are discerning the potential of their call to ministry. I am writing to the ones who think they might benefit from, or enjoy, hearing firsthand experiences, joys, and mistakes of the first few years of ministry, being shared from the perspective of another pastor. I think it helps to hear from someone who has taken the time to share from their own insight, from the files of their own hard-earned wisdom and experiences, written plainly and simply. Hopefully, this material will help you avoid some common pitfalls that are out there waiting for you in ministry. I am even writing to those that may have been around a while and just need a good laugh. Still, you might just benefit from reading it anyway. I have very few initials behind my name, and in no way proclaim to be a great writer. I figure you might applaud or give me an "amen" on that statement later! Prior to the pastoral ministry, I spent most of my career as a healthcare provider or seeing the country from a mobile office that was attached to eighteen wheels. As much as those two careers contrast, they provided much help in my formation in ministry, so do not sell your own background short.

I found that there were many things that I encountered that I would have liked to have been better prepared to handle in the first few years of my own ministry. Utilizing the "seat of the pants" model of learning, although fulfilling, can prove to be most painful! Through this book, you might gain similar insight and hear about some experiences you may not have otherwise considered until you found yourself being drug wildly and unexpectedly by the seat of your pants behind a most unexpected and unpleasant runaway ministry experience. I did not like those types of experiences and do not recommend them to anyone. If this sounds interesting, you might just want to continue ahead! These first months and years will prove very important in your journey. It is no secret that there are many things involved with ministry that you do not know. There will be many things that you don't know that you don't know. You know? Taking it one step further, there are certain areas and situations you are going to encounter and will not know exactly how to ask! I will attempt to write clearly and to the point. I will add some personal experiences along the way to help you gain some perspective. There are no case study reports or group projects contained in this work and I am not going to throw scripture at you. The primary goal is simply to help those considering ministry (*you*) and to supply them with information to help them be more prepared for those first real experiences in pastoral ministry. Sadly, there are no comprehensive texts available that will tell you what to do in most situations.

There will be some scenarios discussed in this book that may indeed help you avert some of the common pitfalls that are incurred in pastoral ministry. These areas will include speaking about those things that cause loss of sleep and premature graying of hair! The scenarios may even help you keep your hair a while longer while keeping you in better standing with your spouse! Moreover, it may even prevent nail-biting and ulcers, but, there is no guarantee written or implied! There are many prayers, processes, and steps, someone may have undergone while exploring a call to ministry. It is imperative that they receive as much support from their peers so they may have every reasonable chance of having a successful and fulfilling ministry experience. If you are still following along and have not kicked me to the curb as a lunatic and idiot, God is good, all the time! The devil is a liar! Let's get to it!

Rev. John L. Vance Ph.D.
Meadow Bridge, WV

Introduction

As a part of their program of study seminaries and divinity schools usually organize themselves into departments, one of which is a department of practical theology. Offering in practical theology include such courses as preaching, counseling, church administration, worship, administration of the sacraments and other rites of the church, such as weddings and funeral, and so on. By designating an academic department as "practical" a distinction is being made between practice and theory, that is, studies that teach us how to do something and how to apply what we know over against those more theoretical disciplines that direct us to reflect on truth and principle, knowledge-oriented subjects such as Biblical studies, theology, church history, and the like.

The ancient Greek philosopher, Aristotle (384-322 B.C.) was one of the first to make this distinction between theory and practice (*theoria* and *praxis*). For him *theoria* was an activity aimed at reflection and truth, while *praxis* was an activity aimed at action and production. Ultimately, for Aristotle, theory (contemplation) was more important, for the philosopher at least.

This distinction may be helpful in understanding some aspects of philosophy and psychology, but such a distinction can never give cause for the church or the believer to separate theory and practice, or even to prefer one activity over the other. This is especially so when it comes to the relationship found in the Bible between doctrine and life. Christian teaching requires its followers to have knowledge of the Lord (to know him), to commit their way to him, and to live for him. For the believer, this is simply a matter of entering more deeply into reality, as to what is true, and good, and beautiful.

For this reason, a minister or pastor who labors in the Lord's vineyard must first be a student of the things God, as the Apostle Paul makes clear: "Study to show thyself approved unto God, a workman that needeth not to be ashamed, rightly dividing the word of truth" (2nd Tim. 2:15). Thus, it follows that one must know something to contribute something. This is a reality that compels the pastor to be a student of the Scriptures, as these Scriptures are read and studied in conversation with the great teachers of the past and present that the Lord has placed in his church. Living and studying within this context, that is, the context of the fellowship of saints (*communio sanctorum*) enables the pastor to learn from God, to hear God's callings, and to receive God's empowerment so that he will be able to rightly proclaim those great salvific truths revealed in Scripture. Such a one forged in the fires of the Lord in this way is a true and effective shepherd of God's flock (see 2nd Tim. 4:1-5, 1st Corinthians 12:28, 2nd Peter 1:19-21). The Rev. Robby Shorter is such a man. He has traveled this path that I have just described.

I want briefly, though, at this point, to step back in time, to a previous period in Robby's life before his call to pastoral work. Back then, Robby was engaged in many other occupations and undertakings that I believe helped him hone some of his God given gifts and talents as a person. He has been a nurse in the past, working in various settings; at one stretch he was an EMS worker; at another, a truck driver, and more, but this will suffice to make my point. I refer to Robby's work history in order to observe that a person's employments and interests have the power to shaped and change that person for the better. In Robby's case I judge that these undertakings have enhanced his ability to appreciate and empathize with people, and his ability to understand the times in which we live (I Chronicles 12:32). These sorts of experiences I believed, helped to prepare Robby for the responsibilities he now shoulders as a pastor of God's people.

I came to know Robby when he was the pastor of the church I now attend; so, I have observed his skills and compassion for people and his pastoral aptitude and manner firsthand. Over the past months, Robby has drawn on these rich experiences to write a book on pastoral ministry that largely focuses on the ministry of the local church. If the reader has followed my drift thus far, he will see that what I have written to this point is meant to serve as a context for my remarks on the work that Robby has written. Therefore, in what follows, I want to provide a brief synopsis of his work and the use that I think it will best serve the church.

This work is designed for and suited, in my opinion, to reach the people in the pews, to speak to those who might be weighing and praying about a call to ministry, to students, and to offer guidance to those pastors who have had little opportunity to engage in formal pastoral studies because of their circumstances in life. As such, it is not filled with the language of the academy, nor is it pitched so high that the ordinary person cannot grasp it. The language is folksy, the work is well illustrated and salted with humor and personal stories. These qualities are liberating in that they allow the reader to relax and enjoy the nuggets of wisdom and counsel contained in it. In brief, this work communicates.

Even more, this is a practical, not a theoretical effort. Nevertheless, the author assumes that those who read its pages believe that Holy Scriptures are the authoritative Word of God, and that the great truths that all genuine Christians have believed, taught, and confessed through the centuries is the teaching of these same Scriptures. Further, this work assumes that the Holy Spirit is powerfully at work in the ministry of the church, through the reading of Scripture through the preaching and teaching of the Gospel, and through the administration of the sacraments. Even more, this author explicitly deals with the Holy Spirit's work of calling, saving, sanctifying, and guiding believers through their relationship to Lord.

What benefit, then, is this book to the reader? Mainly, this work is a manual for pastors, a "how to book," a guide to aid in his work. Those who are not pastors, though, will get a close up and personal look at what the life of a pastor is like, his struggle, temptations, and concerns, as well as a view of the pastor's routine, and how he goes about his duties. But there is more, much more. Robby gives sage counsel on such topics as the administration of baptism and the Lord's Supper, and on performing weddings and funerals, and other such matters. For this writer, trough, the main dish, and this will differ with each reader, was his astute treatment of how to counsel people and how to make effective hospital calls, activities that have to do with shepherding the flock. There is no doubt that some pastors have better people skills than others, as is the case with some doctors and nurses, and others in the help professions. I think Robby's people skills are outstanding, and it shines through in these chapters. Reading this will help improve the poor counselor's skills.

The book also deals with ministry decision making. Robby introduces some concerns and blessing that a person should consider when pondering a call to ministry. He also discusses some very some important topics that are given little space in most academic pastoral theologies, the role of the pastor's spouse, and the necessity of having good pastoral friends and confidents. He addresses the knotty problem of when the pastor should stay or go. All in all, a valuable book filled with prudent counsel and guidance. I recommend it to students and seasoned ministers alike. The student will get a virtual tour of the pastoral ministry; and, for the experienced minister, it will become a *vade mecum*, as the scholars say, a book to carry around with you or to have close at hand to consult.

I found that I was holding my breath, and saying, come on! You can do this! Go for it!

CHAPTER 1

Which Kid Are You?

The world is full of people from different backgrounds and experiences. They are coming from different places and going in different directions. We all come from diverse backgrounds, have different career choices, and enjoy differing levels of education and life experiences. Do you think it is simply a coincidence that our paths are crossing through one great and unmistakable common thread, Jesus Christ? Our experiences and hesitations have certainly and unmistakably brought us to the same point in our lives where we are seeking out and exploring the call into ministry.

After acknowledging the diversity that exists in the climate of our experience and education, I want to entice you further, by suggesting those who are reading this book may find themselves in one of the four categories that follow. In my career and travels, I have had the privilege of meeting and working with some very fine people. We each have different personalities and those personalities make us unique and diverse. The following paragraphs will introduce you to four distinct personality types that I have identified in those people seeking pastoral ministry. Your first challenge is to see if you can recognize or relate to any of the following personalities.

For the past few years it had been very hectic for my wife and me and we found it very difficult to take time off for ourselves, so we seized the opportunity to get away from home and travelled seven hours southeast to the beach. On this day, I had reluctantly agreed to accompany my sweet wife out of a wonderfully air-conditioned room for a quiet walk on the beach and a time of rest at the pool. She loves to walk on the beach very early but I was never one to rise that early while on vacation, or one that liked to waste good air conditioning. I had spent the morning carefully guarding it as well as the coffee pot. Sadly, I am not one of those fortunate souls that get out in the sun and receive a beautiful tan. I am the one you will catch a glimpse out of the corner of your eye scurrying like a sand crab being chased by a seagull, to find the closest shady spot and get out of the sun. I am much more at home in the great outdoors, the woodsy type that can spend hours sitting in a hunting blind, hiking, or standing quietly in a stream fishing. We all know that life is give and take. My wife loves the beach with the same voracity I like the outdoors! We cherish our time together and slow lazy walks on the beach are something my wife really loves and enjoys. It is her happy place and seeing her happy makes me happy. Truthfully, I really love the beach, I just prefer viewing it from about the tenth floor, while drinking coffee, and being in very close proximity to air conditioning. HEY! Don't judge me!

Back to our story. We were seated by the pool after finding suitable shade. I had settled into a comfy chair and began observing the people moving about and happily enjoying the lazy rivers and the various adult and kiddie pools. My attention was averted when my eyes and attention were drawn to this one little fella, who had just arrived at the pool with his mother. He looked to be all of two feet tall, but it was easy to see he was indeed a wild one! His mother was trying desperately to restrain him as she feverishly labored to slather on the necessary amount of sunscreen to prevent him from roasting in the hot sun like a piece of bacon. It was that blue kind too, so he began to resemble a Smurf. The chore of putting water wings on him after the application of the healthy dose of the sunscreen was much like trying to catch greased lightning! He was struggling with the determination of a professional escape artist as he tried to loosen himself from her motherly grip and get himself to the water. After a great and respectable effort, he finally extricated himself from his mother's grip. He squealed loudly and gleefully as he turned about-face and spun out like a pint-sized dragster running on nitrous oxide. He was headed for the pool with impressive speed and agility for a two-foot-tall little boy. His little feet were nothing but a blur! I was waiting for his mother to catch up with him. She possessed neither his agility nor his determination, so she quickly fell behind. I was expecting him to head for the kiddie pool which was located over in the adjacent corner, but was shocked and amazed when he abruptly signaled for, and made, a hard turn to starboard, increased full speed to flank, and headed on a new bearing for the big boy pool! He was not slowing down and his mother was not catching up! I was beginning to contemplate that there might soon arise the need to have to leave my comfortable spot in the shade, don my Johnny

Res-Q hat, and assist with a water rescue. I did not find these thoughts appealing in the least.

About this time, Speedy Gonzales arrived at the edge of the pool and jumped in. *BONZAI*! He flew into the pool at full speed, arms and legs are flailing wildly. He entered the water with a mighty splash, one very large for a boy so small! He was laughing all the way and spluttering joyfully as he went out of sight. The water wings and some blue greasy film was all that remained on the surface of the water where he had just entered. Undoubtedly, they simply slid off his tiny little arms as they were still quite heavily lubricated with sunscreen. I had instinctively arisen from my shady spot and was just about to go fishing for him when his mother arrived at the side of the pool. She was looking straight down into the water and didn't seem to be seeing him. I was not enjoying the thoughts of performing resuscitation on a child, by the pool, at the beach. I was really worried, and about to take a look to see where I needed to jump in to retrieve him when I noticed a flash of color on the other side of the pool. NO! It just couldn't be! But yes, there was Speedy Gonzales, climbing out on the other side of the pool with a grin from ear to ear. I was absolutely flabbergasted at what I had just observed. I could see that his mother's color was strikingly pale, resembling Casper the Ghost. It was my conclusion she was a lot like me and did not care for the sun, or, that we had both witnessed something that neither of us had expected to happen. I think we were both under the presumption that this little fella couldn't swim. The only problem was that Speedy Gonzales didn't seem to be aware of our presumption, or care!

Another time, on another day, a different scenario. I was

sitting by the pool again, in the shade. Are you noticing a pattern yet? This pool had a diving board and was much closer to home. This day found me observing a young boy, about eight years old, on a diving board. He was trying to get up his courage to dive or jump. I quickly realized that I could relate to how he felt. I was in my mid-teen years when I learned to swim. I remembered all too well being afraid to dive into the water. This boy would stand patiently and wait for the other kids to go off the board and then he would climb up there and stand and look into the water. There were a couple of times he sat on the end of the board and just looked longingly into the water. It was not hard to figure out what he was thinking. When children were wanting to dive, he would walk back and get out of their way and allow them to use the diving board. Each time, he would go back and look into the water. We watched as other children did cannonballs, swan dives, watermelons, and every type of maneuver imaginable. These kids were having a really good time and were enjoying just being kids. It was easy to see how badly this one wanted to be like them, but he simply could not muster the courage to take the chance and go for it! I found myself intrigued by this young man and his struggle that day. I found that I was holding my breath, and saying, come on! You can do this! Go for it!

Each time, he would lose his courage and walk off the diving board. I kind of lost interest for a bit and let my mind wander elsewhere, I figure it was to the thought of air conditioning and coffee. I remember that my thoughts had returned to the saga of the little fella on the diving board and happened to look up just in time to see him finally bounce off the end of the board and fly into the sky like an Air Force fighter jet! I watched with surprise and joy as he stretched his arms outward, then suddenly changed his mind, and covered his face. Oh my, I thought, this one was going to be ugly! His contorted frame then assumed, what I can best describe, as the features of someone in a game of Twister gone wrong. In a split second, he contacted the surface of the water with an enormously uncontrolled splash. Oh my, it wasn't pretty and looked quite painful. I watched intently to see if he popped up ok. I recalled vividly clear memories of the little wild boy from the beach. It didn't take but a few seconds to get my answer. He popped up from the water and climbed effortlessly up the ladder onto dry land. It was easy to see that he was now sporting a grin that was touching his ears. I wanted to clap and cheer and celebrate for him. He quietly celebrated his momentous accomplishment, while no one else seemed to notice. He straightaway climbed the ladder and went off the diving board at a full run. It was at that moment, I was aware I had just witnessed a pivotal change occur in this little fella's life. I don't know if his mother or father was watching, but, I noticed that there was a visible and positive difference in him after his wild and uncontrolled splash.

My third story takes me to my hometown. This scenario plays out at a local river near our home. Annually, there are hundreds of local kids that seem to migrate towards this little out of the way place in the summer to swim and frolic. On one side of the river, there is a rock ledge, and many kids, and some adults, climb up that ledge so they can take a jump into the river. The first ledge is about ten feet up. The second one is a good twenty feet and the third level is another five feet higher. I just happened to be passing by the location one day and was watching a group of these kids jump off those ledges into the river. All but one young girl, she appeared to be fifteen or sixteen.

She was much like the young boy I watched on the diving board. All of the other teens were wet from their repeated jumps into the water, however, this young lady was completely dry. She would not jump from any of the ledges despite the cheers from her friends, who were encouraging her to jump. She would walk back and forth looking intently at the water. It was clear, in my mind anyway, that she wanted to jump, however, something kept her from taking that final plunge. Thirty minutes went by, and I kept waiting on one of her friends to lose patience and grab her and push her off the ledge, or take her hand and offer to jump with her. Neither occurred, and she stood by each time and allowed her friends to jump.

They continued to take many turns climbing to the ledges and jumping into the river below. I continued to observe her behavior. She finally climbed down from the ledge and came down to the area below where the other boys and girls were exiting the water. Although she showed great interest in what the others were doing, she couldn't bring herself to jump off of any of the ledges into the refreshing water below. She never took the plunge and was seated with her friends when I finally left the area and headed homeward.

The fourth person is a little different. I was part of a larger group of individuals that were participating in an extensive discernment process for pastoral ministry. The process was complex and included organized group meetings, prayer, and group conversations about our thoughts and feelings regarding our calling to ministry. It was a very heart-warming process that occurred over a few different weekends. It introduced me to a wonderful group of people that I will always consider to be close friends and colleagues. On this particular day, we were seated around the table while each of us took turns talking about why we were there. There was a young lady of about twenty-two, and she sat directly to my right. The process was moving in a circle and we were seated at the end of the circle and the opportunity for us to give our story was now upon us. She was to speak before me, and when she opened her mouth, tears began to flow from her eyes. As her tears began to flow, the Holy Spirit began to touch her heart, and everyone else's too! She spoke these words that I will never forget. They were simple and to the point. She said, *"I don't know why I am here, or, where I am going. I just know that God said I was to be here."* I was in absolute agreement with her, as the power and presence of the Holy Spirit was overwhelming at that moment.

In so many words, I have shared with you how some of us may have approached the wonderful world of ministry. I am not referring to your ministerial calling, I am referring to the journey you may have undergone to get there. You could still be going through it. I view it from the perspective that we are much like those kids that I have been describing in the previous paragraphs. Some of us are so worried about what may happen to us in the journey that we dwell on it and look for every way in the world to talk ourselves out of it, and look for things that will keep us from doing it. There are those of us who know very well that ministry is in us and we find ourselves right there on the edge, ready to go, but always seem to talk ourselves out of actually jumping in. Others finally do it, they jump in, and despite their best efforts it is nowhere near as controlled or engaging as it had been intended. Finally, some people are just like that little wild boy I described in the first part of this chapter. They instinctively seem to know and run straight ahead, trusting Jesus is going to be there. These folks run and fly into the deep end with a splash and swim away like a pro.

WOW! We are at the end of the first chapter! If I have figured it correctly, you are probably laughing right now and thinking about which one of those examples you just identified with. But, what if you did not identify with any of those? I would not worry about that for even a milli-second. When you are ready, and if you dare, let's jump into the next chapter and see what happens.

Please remember that God has already considered all of our issues, faults, and shortcomings long before we even remotely realized that He was calling us into pastoral ministry.

CHAPTER 2

Now What?

This is where it all begins to take shape. Hopefully, you have decided to jump in!

Congratulations to you! Now, what happens? This is the place where many things are going to start happening. Exciting things! Wonderful things! You may be stressed about this but trust that God has this under control. You may be thinking you just made the biggest mistake of your life when you said YES to ministry and wish you had just stayed silent on that particular day you stepped up to answer your call to ministry. You may have already experienced a sickening feeling in the pit of your stomach just thinking about all of the unknowns in your future. Tell the devil to go away, and just keep going! Remember this: You are answering a call to serve God in pastoral ministry and you are answering the call to serve God as He directs you and go where He wants you to go. We cannot serve God when we are putting conditions on how, when, and where we are willing to serve. There is no doubt this will take you out of your comfort zone. God wants you to swim into the deep water where your feet are not able to touch the bottom. He wants you to come out and be totally dependent on Him.

You will be making some choices that will affect your family and its dynamics. Be sure to include your family in the conversations and decisions as much as possible, especially your spouse! Your spouse needs to be on board and feel this too. How are you going to be serving? Will you be part-time? Full-time? ***HINT***: There is no such thing as being a "*part-time*" shepherd. You will learn that you will have full-time expectations in your duties and obligations, even though you may be paid part-time because the church cannot support you full time. There are going to be weeks that you will have worked forty hours on your secular job and made a half dozen visitations in the evenings. You will have studied and gotten your sermon almost ready, but when Sister Gail calls at midnight and tells you momma is in the hospital and wants her pastor, you can't say that you are part-time and cannot go. Instead, you jump up and go comfort momma. You may be serving in a church where you do not receive a salary. Instead, you may receive love offerings while supporting yourself and your family as a bi-vocational pastor. The term bi-vocational means you work a secular job and pastor at the same time. Expectations will still be the same. Will you be relocating? Will you be moving into a parsonage? Will your family be relocating with you? That last sentence may sound strange, but it is not. For five years, my wife and I have shared two homes. Her job covers us with insurance allowing me the freedom to take care of pastoral needs when the congregation could not afford to cover us. The downside for us is that we are not always together during the week. It was not what we really wanted, however, it was what was needed. These are some of the things that will be being considered as you move forward into the future as a pastor.

Many will become stressed because they feel that they "*don't know enough*" to be a pastor and you are probably correct. The truth is you will *NEVER* know enough. You will be studying God's Word for the remainder of your life and at the end of it, you still won't know it all. Please remember that God has already considered all of our issues, faults, and shortcomings long before we even remotely realized that He was calling us into pastoral ministry. You can trust that his grace is sufficient! Remember, God does not call the equipped, but equips the called! There is something special that I really want to share with you. I had concerns and worries just like everyone else does when considering ministry. I noticed a personal spiritual comfort as I began to care for the congregation. I realized that I been distressed about how ministry was going to affect my situation and had not considered how my answering the call to ministry was affecting all of those families I had been called to serve. It is humbling because you realize that you were not looking at the bigger picture. God always sees the bigger picture!

I began my pastoral ministry in a large denomination. I went through a process of discernment and attended their licensing school. I had a fantastic instructor named Monty Brown and he had authored the book being used for his class. The name of the book is *Free Us for Joyful Obedience: A Primer on Pastoral Caregiving from a Pastor's Heart.* (*ISBN # 9781425980122*) I read his book with great enthusiasm during the pre-course preparation and found it as one of the most helpful and meaningful books that I have had the privilege of reading. It is an excellent read and I recommend it for your library. Monty wrote something in that book that has stayed with me. I share this with his blessing and permission. It has become embedded as a fixture in my spiritual foundation. He explained that there are three main rules for pastoral ministry. The first rule was *"Love your people."* The second rule was *"Love your people."* The third rule was *"Love your people."* This is going to prove to be true in your own ministry. There will be times you will not know what to say to them. Love your people! There will be times you find that you may want to strangle them or they may want to strangle you! Love your people! There will be times the leadership or membership may have seemingly lost the cheese off the cracker and established some very unrealistic or unreachable goals for you that Superman couldn't attain on his best day. Love your people! I reach out to Monty about six months into my first appointment and shared with him how those three rules had proven themselves a positive influence in my life when I wasn't exactly sure what my next move should be.

There are two prominent themes of pastoral ministry, loving and serving. Being a minister and a servant requires both desire and effort. You are going to have to allow yourself to be stretched. Pastors need to be available to their parishioners and need to be prepared to lead them through whatever issues they are facing. Those that choose to enter ministry with a feeling that they do not have to serve and love the people will find quickly that they do not belong in pastoral ministry.

Furthering and enhancing your education will be something that will be addressed at some point as you begin your journey. Depending on your situation or church background you may already be in seminary or taking some type of pastoral education classes. Look forward to furthering your education as a pastor! There is much you will want to know and understand so you can fully and confidently help your people understand who they are in Christ and how they can grow in their faith. A little friendly advice on this point. First, wherever you go for your education, you may find it a challenge listening and agreeing when instructors say something that may be contrary to what you may personally believe or practice. Don't get bent out of shape over it! Being stretched and challenged is not a bad thing! You may find it to be a benefit when you have to dig down deep and find and support scripturally why you believe what you believe. You may find that some of the things you believed were from something you heard or understood incorrectly, and when you get right down to it, find you must change your perspective. I think I am safe in saying that this happens to all of us at some point. You will encounter different theological perspectives and will see just how diverse and different are those that call themselves Christians; how belief and worship can differ. There is so much more for you to learn about where we are as a society and the events that have led up to how we got there. Some of this is not specifically addressed and answered in the Bible. It can, however, be learned in biblical history and studying the writings of biblical scholars.

There is much more about the church in the bigger picture that you will need to learn and understand as you transform and grow in your ministry. You will be grateful that you learned about events in our history such as the

Protestant Reformation. You must learn about people like Augustine, Martin Luther, John Calvin, John Wesley, Huldrych Zwingli, and Phineas Bresee. You will appreciate that you studied and became familiar with matters like the Wesleyan Quadrilateral or the Great Spiritual Awakening of the 1800s. You will begin to see that the shepherd is leading the flock and watching out for them and nurturing them as the flock eats and grows. You are seeing to it that they have a healthy diet that is rich in spiritual nutrition, and to do that, you must understand where they are coming from and how they got there.

You will learn how the sacraments of baptism and communion, as well as why some parts of our worship, may be different depending on what theological perspective the church follows and supports. Trust me when I say that in time you will appreciate all of this. Maybe not while you are going through it, but you will appreciate it later!

Let us recap a few things about what comes next after you say YES to pastoral ministry. You are saying yes to God and His will for you. You will be stepping into the waters of ministry in one of several levels of commitment. You will be making decisions that are going to affect your family. You are going to be placed with a church that is full of new people that are going to need love, care, and patience, and you may not know any of them! You are going to be called upon to serve these people in many ways that you may have never considered. You are going to be praying for them, praying with them, leading them, teaching them, counseling them, performing their marriages, baptizing them, presiding at their funerals, and supporting them through some of the greatest and worst times of their lives. To accomplish this successfully, you are going to need the benefit of some important things. First, you need to hold tight and listen to God for his leading. Second, you will need to have a solid prayer life. And third, you will need some form of pastoral education and guidance. Just remember, love your people, serve your people, and trust in God and his sufficient grace!

"Do you mow grass?"

CHAPTER 3

There is a New Pastor in Town!

There may be some of you that have already surpassed those first pages and find yourself at this location on the ministry map. You may have already made those difficult decisions with your family and maybe serving at your new church. Welcome! There may be some of you that started with me at the beginning that is now heavily considering becoming an over the road truck driver after reading the last chapter. Don't lose your faith in God or let that previous chapter discourage you!

I was immensely thankful that my initial preparations for pastoral ministry were very well organized with plenty of support in the initial phases. I remember what it was like when I arrived at my first full-time appointment. Our Bishop had assigned me to serve four churches. Yes, you heard it correctly, FOUR CHURCHES. I remember very well the evening that my wife and I were scheduled to meet the pastoral relations committee. We were driving from our home to meet them. It was about fifty miles from our home and we were about two-thirds of the way there when my sweet wife asked a question that I had somehow overlooked. She looked at me and asked, *"Are you nervous?"* I was surprised at the question, and while thinking about it for a moment, realized that I had not spent a lot of time being nervous. I answered, *"No, should I be nervous?"* Great, now I *was* nervous! Suddenly, I began to formulate in my mind all of the possibilities and the endless scenarios that may very shortly confront me. Okay, now what? Trust God. Remember that passage "Greater is He that is in you than he that is in the world?" That really is true.

My District Superintendent met us at the church and accompanied us into that evening's meeting. It was a very warm group of people that were just looking for someone that would love them and treat them with care and respect. They were doing their best to make us feel welcome and comfortable as we came in and sat down with them. As we began to formally engage in conversation there was one gentleman, about seventy years old, that got up from his chair and, without introducing himself, stated that he had *"One question only."* Oh my, here it comes! I knew that I was about to get the big one right out of the gate and, was confident this one was going to be a doozy. I could feel it, he is going to ask me a deep theological question. He was a solidly built man that had a stern disposition and a very firm facial expression. There did not seem to be an ounce of foolishness in him and his hands reflected many years of hard labor. My stomach became queasy almost immediately. Now it hit me, why hadn't I thought this through a little more before this meeting? I was going to look like a fool, I just knew it! Here it comes! He looked me square in the face and asked, *"Do you mow grass?"*

Admittedly, I didn't see that one coming. I regained my thoughts and felt the abrupt onset of nausea and worry leave. I immediately responded with a smile that I was quite proficient with almost all of the hand tools and equipment that pertained to mowing and lawn care. I assured him I was very experienced in their application and usage. I threw in for good measure that I was even good at taking out the trash, and had even been known to do windows in a pinch. He responded, "*OK, I'm good*" and he sat down, seemingly relieved his personally important question was addressed.

The next question I was asked, I am still trying to answer five years later. A very sweet lady asked me, "*What is your passion?*" A very credible, personal, and honest question! I thought pastoring and ministry was my passion, however, it didn't seem to be the answer she may have been seeking. If I ever figure it out, I plan to call her and tell her that I finally figured out an answer to her question. She was very good to my wife and me while we were serving there and her kindness will never be forgotten.

There is a good point to be made here. People will be willing to accept you as the new kid on the block. They will want to get to know you, learn what makes you tick. I was a man that grew up using tools and getting my hands dirty. My lawn care question came from a man that had always known hard manual labor and wanted to know if I was someone that would be willing to pull my weight and labor along with them. As the days went by this man and his wife became great supporters of our ministry, and his family became wonderful and faithful friends to us. My advice is to try to be yourself and try to learn and understand the setting you are entering into. Do not make the mistake of trying to be what you think they want you to be!

If you do that you are going to cheat yourself and you are going to cheat them. Let them get to know that wonderful person that God is sending them to lead them and be their pastor! A warm smile and a presentation of a loving and caring spirit with a heart of love is a great start. Remember, Love your people and show them you are willing to serve their needs as their pastor. In this case, you are helping them grow and trust God. Remember this one important point. They were praying for a pastor to be sent just as hard you were praying about becoming one!

Concerning you being the new kid on the block, everyone in town is going to know that you are the new pastor and they will be watching your every move. They will be listening to your sermons and teaching very carefully. Many people not attending your church are going to be watching and talking about you! You will be at a disadvantage for a while as you learn your way. Don't be surprised or dismayed if people aren't immediately coming to you with open arms. For a while, you will be compared to the previous pastor. That could be a good thing and it could be a challenging issue.

Be gracious in your first steps! It can be especially difficult if the previous pastor was beloved by the congregation. You may have to help them heal from the loss of their previous pastor in your first weeks and months. Although difficult, helping them see that you care enough about them to allow them this time to grieve over their loss shows that you are here for them and not just your own precious ego. You may encounter exactly the opposite! You may be coming in behind a pastor that didn't have a good relationship with the church, so there may be some healing needed regarding trust and leadership issues. You may find that your church family could be making their way through some very broken and painful experiences that occurred in the church and that overflowed into the community. There could be some significant spiritual wounds that will need your careful attention and care. Be gracious to their position, and try not to take it personally.

Try to make yourself available to meet people in the community and outside the doors of your church. **HINT.** Take time to get a shirt or jacket that has your name and the church name on it. When you are in the community, it is an easy reference for people to know the church family you represent and also to know your name. Further, be sure to look the part of the pastor. There is a tendency today to dress casually. I believe it is important for a pastor to always look the part when performing pastoral duties. It doesn't have to be a suit and tie or a formal dress, but people in the community still have ideas about what a pastor should look like. Once you are there, your leadership may suggest your dress, and that is fine. If you have someone show up at church on Sunday they will most likely identify you first as pastor by your dress and demeanor. It is a good idea to get out and work around the parsonage and around the church in work attire. Let them see you are not afraid to get your hands dirty. This allows them to see you dressed in formal and casual dress. Also, be looking for and listening for cues that will help you be able to feel the pulse of the heartbeat in the community.

Let's recap. Be yourself! Just as you are learning the

congregation, the congregation will be trying to get to know and learn who you are too! Let the love of God show through you. You must realize that just as you are praying about being the shepherd, the flock is praying also about the one that will come and be their leader. Dress and act the part! Get to know your people and learn what is important to them. You may find that you were prematurely stressed for no reason. I realized quickly that sometimes perceptions and needs of church people can be very straightforward and simple. In the case of my lawn care person, he was just wanting to know that I was willing to pitch in get my hands dirty. Let them see that God has sent them the right pastor and servant for the job. Be willing to pitch in and get your hands dirty!

Leadership has a face. Leadership has qualities. They will be watching you carefully while they unknowingly begin to trace the characteristics and features of your face into their understanding of what their new leadership will look like. Author

CHAPTER 4

On Your Mark! Get Set!
Wait a Minute!

It was about three months into my current pastoral position, I had relocated to a new area and am now serving in a different denomination that allows me to serve one church family. It was a beautiful Sunday morning and I was making my morning visit upstairs to where our children were located. I look forward to going up and visiting them while they are still eating their snack. I typically try to be out front to welcome them when the church van arrives. Our church calls it a snack because we do not want any of the children to think that some of their friends may not have eaten before getting to church. It is always a highlight of the morning to spend time with them and spend a few minutes getting a high five and a hug here and there. I sincerely look forward to it every Sunday, and truthfully, the kids don't seem to mind it either. I am serving in an area that has suffered over the years with the economic downturn. Sadly there is a distinct poverty issue and along with it is the problem with substance abuse and alcoholism. The kids are the ones that seem to suffer the worst. We do our best to help when and how we can.

As I came back down to the sanctuary to begin greeting those arriving for worship, I was told by one of my parishioners that I needed to be on my best behavior this morning because we had visitors. When I looked up, I recognized two smiling faces that I knew well. They were very frequent attendees from my last appointment. They were not members, but in actuality, were more dedicated than some of those that were members. They are siblings and often travel together and they had promised me that one day they would visit me at my new church. They were fulfilling that promise on this day. One is a minister of a different denomination, and we are wonderful friends and love each other dearly in the Lord. We always have some wonderful conversations and respect one another's gifts. They invited my wife and me to join them after the service and be their guests at lunch. We were happy to accept and spend that time with them.

While we were enjoying our time at lunch, it was mentioned that my wife and I looked very different since they last were with us, and commented that we seemed to have lost weight, adding that we looked wonderful. I laughed and replied that, unfortunately, I had not lost weight, but thanked her for that compliment. My wife chimed in with a similar laugh and a similar response. We enjoyed a wonderful reunion and an hour-long lunch. Hugs were shared and prayers for God's continued grace in both of our lives. Before their departure that afternoon, the minister spoke up again and shared with us that the Lord had revealed during our visit that the appearance that they had associated with weight loss was really a loss of the weight of stress and worry. It made sense. We had left a tremendous weight behind us when we moved. We dearly loved those people but the three churches were proving an insurmountable task and more than we could physically, mentally, and spiritually take. It was immediately apparent to her that there was something different about us when they saw us after only about three months.

It wasn't that we were not happy beforehand, but that we seemed at peace, shalom. If you caught it earlier, I had said that I was pastoring four churches in the beginning. One church was forced to close during my first year and as a result, left me with three. Good catch!

It is my opinion that this is one of the most important chapters of this book. Please read it very thoughtfully and carefully. Before you get immersed in all of the details of the ministry and living the life of a pastor, I want to address something that holds extreme importance, and that is your own care! What exactly does this mean? It means you are human and not super-human. You still need all of the same things that any of your church people need to live a healthy and happy life. This includes proper food, rest, and care for your own body and soul. This includes the care of your spouse and your children. They will be affected by every aspect of your work.

I began working in EMS at a young age. I clearly remember being taught in my many classes that the first person that should be looked after, was the rescuer. The rescuer is useless if they do not protect themselves. As a matter of fact, in some of those testing scenarios, failing to address the safety or protection of the rescuer was one of the criteria that was an automatic failure of that scenario. There are so many things that are involved in ministry that you cannot get it all done in one day, one week, one year, or one lifetime. You have to be the pastor and this means leading and this means serving. It does not mean that you are required to personally carry out the mission for the entire church. That sounds like an obvious statement now, but, give it a few months, and then come back and re-read this chapter. You simply cannot be everything for everyone!

A day off. A vacation. Take them when you can! This seems like another one of those no brains necessary type statements, but I have included it in here for a reason. You will come to understand very quickly that ministry can be very consuming. There have been many cases where pastors have found it so consuming that they have inadvertently ignored themselves, their family, and their health. You will be juggling sermon preparation, hospital visitation, home visitation, prayer time, study time, office hours, scheduled meetings, unscheduled meetings, and if you are taking educational classes, you will be preparing and studying for those classes as well. Days can really fly by and you will be getting into bed completely worn out and unable to remember exactly what you have accomplished that day. Do you believe that Jesus wants us to do that? I think the scripture tells us something very different.

You will need to remember that you must take time off from this lifestyle to rest and to take care of yourself. Your family will need time off too. You will find that many people will expect you to be there for them 24/7. Remember, you can't be all things for everybody. The quicker you understand that, the better you will be. I am not saying that you should treat ministry as a nine to five job because we know that ministry is much more than that, but, you must use wisdom in how you manage your time. You must observe a day of rest just as you preach it to your congregation. Be aware of how much time you are giving and serving. Your family needs you too, and you simply must make time to be with them. You need family time together that does not include the church. You will see that it doesn't take long for your new life to be affected by the needs and duties of the church. It is understood and expected you will be excited and happy that you are functioning in your new role since it is a role you have been praying about for some time, right? You must work with your church leadership to establish and maintain healthy boundaries that will allow you to be effective in your roles as a pastor, spouse, and parent. You want to be just as happy and excited when you reach the milestone of five years in ministry, and then ten years, operating with the same vigor you had at the onset of your ministry.

Do you have a hobby? Maybe this is a great time to invest in your spiritual health with a healthy hobby like walking, bicycling, or playing golf. Get the family involved too! Get involved in something that can allow you to burn off the physical and mental calories and evaporate some of the stress that comes with your duties, and create some quality family time too. My family physician once had a message on his office sign that said: *"Nobody ever got depressed riding a bicycle."* I do not know who first coined the phrase; however, it would be worth a try, would it not? Oh, that person who said that you never forget how to ride a bike, well, I proved that they were wrong! That is another story.

Prayer. This is undoubtedly the most effective and important tool you will have in your ministry toolbox and you must not allow the enemy to steal your time of prayer and intercession.

You will use this tool in many aspects and areas of your ministry. You have undoubtedly been doing a lot of praying to get to this point of your life, but more will be required! It is an absolute must that you set aside time to pray for yourself, your family, your ministry, your church, your community, and the list will grow as you go. Hours, days, and a week can fly by before you know it. We can set up a schedule that looks absolutely wonderful on paper but you will learn that an unscheduled call for help can surely change the dynamics of a day in a hurry! Let me share a fictional story with you that was shared with me by my former District Superintendent. I can't remember exactly how she told me the story, but, the point is what is critical.

A man named Sam lived in a small town. He loved where he lived and he loved his town. He was always helping others whenever the opportunity presented. He took great pride in caring for his home and was meticulous in maintaining the yard and garden. He was always looking to make improvements and do things that would improve his property. He had one big issue that he could not overcome, and that was a large rock that was in the front of his yard next to the street. He hated that rock and dreamed of getting it removed. He didn't have the money to pay someone to remove it for him and its continued presence in his yard was always a burden on his mind.

One day a church friend told Sam that he intended to build a new home in the coming year. It would be about a half-mile out of town but he needed to find some way to fill in some of his low-lying lands and was going to be trying to find dirt and debris that could help him in this efforts. Sam immediately thought of his rock and asked the friend, if he could manage to move it, could he bring his rock, his *"burden,"* and rid himself of it forever. The friend happily informed Sam that he could indeed bring that rock over to the property. Sam was ecstatic and began to work diligently to find a way to get that rock out of his yard. He worked and worked to dig out around his rock and one day found that he could move it with a steel bar. He worked for two days and finally managed to turn the rock upon its edge. He realized that he could probably manage to get that rock onto his small wagon and then use his lawn tractor to get that rock out of his life forever. He now had a plan! He was simply overjoyed beyond words.

Early the next morning, before the sun was fully up, Sam was out front with his lawnmower and wagon. After much sweat and physical effort, he managed to load that rock onto his trailer. What a sight it was to behold. He was already imagining the possibilities of how he would tend that area in the future. He began to slowly ease the lawnmower forward and was smiling ear to ear when the old rock began to move away from its former home. Every foot he moved made his smile grow larger. Slowly and steadily he continued towards his friend's property. It was going to take quite a while to get there because he moved very slowly, as the rock, after all, was very heavy.

Sam was about ten minutes into this long-awaited journey when a lady he knew well flagged him down and inquired as to what he was doing. She saw the large rock

and asked if that was the rock from his yard. He replied
with a smile that it was. She asked Sam if he would carry a
rock for her too, as his friend had also informed her of his
intentions. Before he thought, he agreed to do that task and
carried another good-sized rock and added it to his trailer,
and resumed his journey. He was stopped a few minutes
later with another similar request to add a third rock. By the
time he got to the edge of town, he had been stopped three
more times and each time another rock was added. His poor
mower was now complaining at the additional weight and it
was obvious that it was struggling terribly to move forward.
Its tires were sagging precariously low and appeared ready
to pop at any second. There was a small hill ahead and the
final destination was just on the other side of it. The mower
abruptly ground to a wheezy halt about halfway up the small
hill and refused to move an inch further. Sam actually got
behind the mower and tried his best to push the mower to
help get up the hill but without success. He tried everything
he knew but the mower would not go. Cars drove by people
that recognized him passed without stopping to help. Sam
tried and tried but soon found himself exhausted and finally,
and dejectedly, sat down in despair. He cried out to God and
complained loudly. In his despair, he cried, *"Why did you put
such a burden on me, God?"* He sat and wiped the sweat from
his face and lamented his condition and continued to blame
God for his problem. *"Why are you not helping me God?"* He
was still sitting silently contemplating his next move when
he heard a small quiet voice speak inside him. *"Sam, I only
gave you the one rock to deal with."*

Let's recap this chapter. Remember, you are important!
Be sure you take good care of yourself. If you want to be

fired up for the long term and be there for those in your congregation, you must take the necessary steps to develop good self-care habits. And don't be so quick to take on everyone else's rocks!

Our job is to preach the good news. Give them Jesus.
Give them hope. Share Jesus.
Share hope. Preach the path to salvation! Author

CHAPTER 5

The View is Different from the Pulpit

The preacher-the pastor. We are finally arriving at a moment that you have been waiting for while graciously and patiently enduring. Preaching. Let's say it again with emphasis. We are P R E A C H I N G the Word of God! Hallelujah! Praise His Holy Name!

I have kept sermons that I have written and usually save them on the computer or thumb drive, titled and labeled for the year. I kept the first couple of years of ministry in a three-ring binder and learned that the task was too difficult. I learned really early in my ministry that it gave more respect to the congregation to use written notes during sermon delivery. If I chose to preach extemporaneously I knew that I faced the challenge of losing my train of thought and then journey off down the legendary rabbit trail, and then more than likely, I would end up lost down the rabbit hole. It is embarrassing to lose your place in the middle of a sermon.

I have a great friend, one of those more like a sibling, and he did not understand my style of preaching from notes. He had visited one weekend and attended service with me. He was an extemporaneous speaker and shared that he didn't think my current style allowed you the same freedom to flow in the Spirit and be spontaneous. He was a greater believer in extemporaneous preaching and letting the Spirit guide him. Having begun preaching in a charismatic environment and preaching in the same style, I admit that it was hard adapting to this style, however, once I persevered and became comfortable with it I found the same spontaneity as before. It was also very important in my situation to stay on a timeline. It is very embarrassing to lose one's place during a sermon and I think that it is a more common occurrence in extemporaneous preaching. I think that any pastor being honest will tell you if it hasn't happened to them yet, that it will.

In my first appointment, I had to maintain a rigid time table to be sure I arrived at each of the three churches promptly. I needed not to stray too far from the path when preaching. I wasn't always successful at it and arrived late more than a few times. Thank God for his grace, and the spirit of understanding and acceptance on the part of those churches. We never want to rush what God has in store for a service but we also do not want to be irresponsible and recklessly utilize the time we have been given.

I will occasionally look back at, and re-read some of my old sermons. I have read some of them and thought to myself, *"Did I preach this? What was I thinking?"* As time goes by, your understanding of scripture will improve. You will incur depth to your thinking and reasoning. You will search and research and come to understand more about passages of scripture you preach from. I am not trying to imply that anyone's knowledge is lacking, however, I do believe that as you begin this new chapter in your life, you will develop some new habits and, along with it, one of those habits will be how you read and study. I have actually brought up some of my old sermons and rewrote and preached them again using the knowledge I have gained since the first time they were written. Truthfully, it was a mental boost for me to see how I had grown spiritually.

Most pastors will tell you that Sundays and preaching the sermon is a highlight of their week. They will also tell you that challenges faced in the other work that can go along with being a pastor can make it difficult at times to enjoy that preaching. I have difficulty sleeping on Saturday night because I am always looking forward to the service on Sunday. Some may confide to you that they chose the path of the evangelist because they did not feel that they could thrive in pastoral ministry. They love the aspect of preaching but like to be able to preach the sermon and move on to the next service.

My first year being a supply pastor had some difficulties, but it was amazing. In my first preaching assignment, I was assigned to two small rural churches located twelve miles apart. The journey from home to the first church was forty-eight miles. My wife and I would drive a hundred and twenty miles each Sunday while we served those two church families. They were wonderful people and we loved every minute of time we spent with them! We still consider them great friends. We both stood in amazement at how the same sermon notes would yield a completely different type of sermon at each church. It was the first time I preached two sermons in different locations on the same day. We were so enthralled at how this process worked. God is so amazing! If you are just starting to get in the swing of writing a sermon, don't worry! God knows what he will say. Maybe you are dreading that you will be trying to write a sermon every Sunday. Read the sentence again, don't worry, God knows what he will say! Just do your due diligence. Pray, read, pray some more, read some more, pray some more. Think about what you have read, how did it speak to you? Let it steep for a while in your mind, sleep on it, and think about it. What do you feel God is telling you?

Sometimes we will all have extremely difficult weeks and this will affect each of us differently as we work a secular job and pastor. Consider this, God knows your background and can use the background knowledge in your preaching! He used my background in healthcare in many instances to relate to the congregation. I expect you may find it could be similar for you. I would strongly encourage you to never create a sermon around an experience that angered you, or was a result of something that occurred while dealing with a church issue. There is nothing that will quench a service any quicker than the "thou shalt not do that" sermon. You will think you are being slick, but, everyone else will have it figured out within the first five minutes, then spend the rest of the sermon laughing as they figured out who the offender might have been. Don't go there!

I remember this one particularly difficult week, I had studied long and hard and had finally put together the sermon. It was actually printed and lying in front of me but it just didn't feel right. Saturday night had very quickly arrived and the hour was now becoming very late. A lot of effort was in this sermon and I had studied hard to get it where it was, but it just didn't feel right. I did not like the feeling I was having but it was the twenty-third hour and past time for bed. Finally, I called it a night, gave it to God, and went to sleep. The next morning we began the weekly journey to preach the gospel. I was sweating profusely during the drive and my wife could sense what I was feeling. I prayed the entire trip up the West Virginia Turnpike to our destination. We always left home extra early and were always the first ones to arrive at the church. We would usually arrive a half-hour before the start of the service and would have the privilege of opening up the church. We would also have a few minutes of quiet time in the presence of God before the people arrived and the services began. That morning, I walked up to the door of the fellowship hall and was putting my key into the door when it suddenly felt like a river of peace washed over my head. It was as if my mind was a thumb drive and I had just plugged it into God's computer; the message began to download into my heart. I remember looking at my wife and telling her, "*I have it now. God just gave it to me*" Never doubt God!

I am not going to get deep into the building of a sermon. You are going to establish your own method and develop your own way. I will say that you absolutely must spend time reading and studying. It will take time as you begin to take those first steps in sermon building. Today we have a myriad of online tools that will allow you to search endlessly for the material. I suggest that you try to search within the pathway of the theological perspective that you are preaching. If this is unclear, I am referring to the fact that some material will emphasize some biblical areas differently depending on the background and theological perspective of the writer. I want to add something else here. As you are getting started I want to offer you another thought.

Do not overthink! You are beginning, or, accepting a deeper commitment to ministry. The tendency is to overthink and stress about your sermons.

This is a good place for a fictional story about overthinking. A young pastor was born and raised in the southern part of Florida. He was a bright, intelligent young man with a love of God in his heart and a roaring fire deep in his bones. One day he asked his wife if she would be willing to move somewhere that had the beauty of four distinct seasons. He thought he would love being in a place that enjoyed snow each year. He loved the snow and he loved Florida, but, he knew the chances of a beautiful deep snow in south Florida was probably not going to happen. His wife agreed to be supportive of his request so he began to earnestly pray about a possible move in ministry. He learned that there was a church of the same denomination that had an opening for a pastor in a nice town in Montana. He made the necessary contacts and it was offered for him to come and visit the church so they could meet with him, hear him preach, and meet his wife. The church congregation was very pleased with the meeting and after a time of mutual prayer, he was offered the position as their pastor. It was an answered prayer and he quickly and happily accepted the offer. He was ecstatic and was packed and ready to begin the journey when move time arrived. The current church family was sad, however, understood where his heart was leading him and stood by his decision to relocate. They were happy to be a blessing in his next chapter of ministry.

He arrived in Montana in mid-summer and was delighted at the beauty of the scenery he beheld and he eagerly anticipating the four seasons displaying God's glory. He could hardly wait for the first cool night announcing fall. As late August and early September approached the air took on a brisk nature and there was no hiding his smile. Late September arrived with cold air, frost, and some snow flurries. The first week of October found him seated at the table reading the morning paper when he heard an announcement over the radio that the weather forecast was calling for a foot of snow in the coming evening and all residents were asked to park their vehicles on the odd-numbered side of the streets to allow the snowplow adequate room to make a clean sweep. He jumped up from the table immediately and moved his car to the odd side of the street. Sure enough, there were thirteen inches of snow on the ground the next morning. He had been up most of the night watching the beautiful display of snow as if fell in the majesty of Montana. He was at peace. Shalom.

Three days later, this same pastor was up early in the morning and sitting at the breakfast table reading the paper. He was still ecstatic and enjoying the beautiful snow blanketing his town when the radio again announced that another foot of snow was in the immediate forecast and all residents were asked to move their cars to the even-numbered side of the street so the snowplows could get another clean sweep as the additional snow fell. He once again jumped up and moved his car to the even side of the street. As the night fell, the young pastor patiently sat and watched with awe as more snow fell from the sky like puffy balls of cotton and blanketed the region as far as his eye could see. God's majesty had left him speechless.

The week passed and the weekend arrived. The new pastor shared with his congregation his enthusiasm for the beauty of his new home. His personality and vigor brought much joy to his parishioners. They had not met anyone like him in a long time, and it was exactly what they needed! Although they saw snow in a completely different way, they saw something in him that renewed their faith and drew them closer to him. There was just something about him that they could not put their finger on and it encouraged them tremendously. Monday morning found him sleeping a little later than usual since he had been up many hours watching the snowfall the previous week. He was entering the kitchen sleepy-eyed and attempting to shake himself awake. He was pouring his coffee and looking for the newspaper when the faithful radio broadcast announced that there would be another eight inches of snow to fall today and the residents should park their cars on the - ** There was a popping sound in the radio and then silence! The power flickered off in the home and the young pastor immediately became frantic. He completely ignored the fact the power was out. Where was he supposed to park the car? He was getting more frantic by the second, he needed to know! He did not want to impede the snowplow! He was picking up the phone to call one of his parishioners when his wife lovingly handed him his newspaper, and politely removed the phone from his hand. She placed it back into the base, because, it wouldn't have worked anyway since the power was out! She kissed him lightly on the cheek and hugged him sweetly, and then she said these words to him:

"Honey, I think you can leave the car in the garage this time."
Don't overthink the situation!

I would advise you to keep it simple at first, liken your sermons to an old country boy's diet of meat and potatoes. A meal can be designed at any time around meat and potatoes, and so can a sermon. I am sure you understand what meat and potatoes are in scripture. Our job is not to fix people. Our job is to preach the good news. Give them Jesus. Give them hope. Share Jesus.

Share hope. Preach the path to salvation! Everything else can build from there as you go. Sometimes, God will reveal amazing things to you through your study of scripture. It will motivate and inspire you, and it is natural to want to preach it immediately, but, you will find that your congregation is still needing the basic diet of meat and potatoes for now. They will have to wait until their spiritual stomachs can digest more complex food. Follow me?

It will take you some time to gain the proficiency of setting down and putting it all together, but, you will, I promise! In a reasonable time you will be capable of creating a sermon series and write more intricate sermons. I am sorry if you feel as if you have just been punched in the gut. Five chapters to finally get to this and then be told that you aren't going to get deep into preaching? Really? Yes! You are a called preacher and pastor. Trust me when I tell you that God is going to use you in fantastic ways for His glory! I am trying to help you with some of the areas that are lesser discussed that you will have the privilege of experiencing along your way.

Pray with purpose. I recommend that any pastor establish a specific area for prayer whether it be your office, parsonage, or home. You must develop a location that is used for one thing and this one thing only. There was a movie a few years back that introduced many to the idea of a set-aside area of prayer. In that area, you are in communion with God. It can be called your happy place, your safe place, your sanity seat, you name it. But it will most certainly prove beneficial to you. The more time you spend there, the more time you will find that you desire and long to spend there. When you designate this one area as a prayer room, you will soon see and feel that your mindset changes whenever you go in there. One of the issues that we have as pastors is that we are constantly dealing with all types of communication and data flowing into our minds. Being able to unplug, and designate the special time that is designated toward the goal of seeking God and his leadership for your congregation, is priceless. There you can shut out the world, turn off the noise, silence the clamor. There you commune with God. There you will find strength and power.

"The effective leader is the one that leads in such a way that the followers are following without realizing the leader is leading." Mike Goode, Chief, Pineville FD

CHAPTER 6

The Pastoral Leader

Among the many different hats, you will be privileged to wear in ministry, one of the most honored is the one that identifies you as a leader of your church. This is such an awesome and honorable position. You will be stepping into this position knowing that you have a lot to learn. Leadership styles are different and each person leads differently and has their own leadership style, their own area of expertise, strengths and weaknesses. This chapter is about being a leader and not an administrator.

Your church family will be looking intently to see how you lead. You must be able to demonstrate to them that you are not only interested in being their leader, but, know how to lead. You will be leading them in worship, leading them in prayer, and teaching them about living a life of faith. They will be watching you intently for a while until they can be assured that you are capable of leading. Leadership has a face. Leadership has qualities. They will be watching you carefully while they unknowingly begin to trace the characteristics and features of your face into their understanding of what their new leadership will look like. I want to take a moment and instill in your mind the mental picture of a leader.

I want to offer a reflection from one of the leadership classes I attended during my education and draw for you the mental picture of this wonderful leader. This instructor was one of a kind! He was an exceptionally humble man with a wonderful attitude. He maintained a classroom atmosphere that was extremely encouraging and conducive to learning. He had the appearance of everyone's favorite grandfather. When he arrived in class, he appeared as if he had just come home from the office and was about to sit down with the family to a warm fire and a warm beverage. He was wise beyond his years and had a smile that was infectious and his demeanor reflected his knowledge. When he spoke to the class, it was obvious he was a natural leader. His voice never rose, yet, when he spoke it seemed that every eye immediately found him in the room. His class was one of the best I had the pleasure of attending during my time at that learning institution. It was immediately apparent to all that he loved teaching and he loved the learning process. He genuinely enjoyed working with the students in his class and went to great lengths to provide a great learning experience. Are you getting the picture?

A memorable class assignment was writing a paper that addressed different styles of leadership. We were asked to compare our leadership style with that of John Wesley, who, was a key figure in the textbook and class. He was known to be a great leader, one who could preach a sermon among the most intelligent and affluent, go two blocks away and speak to, and relate just as easily, to the downtrodden and simplest members of society. He was an accomplished leader. It was through his abilities of leading others that a movement would soon begin and later be known as the Methodist movement. It was said that Wesley could lead from the side, the center, the front, or the back of any situation. It didn't matter the position, Wesley was able to adapt and successfully and effectively lead from any place he may have found himself at the time. I am sure you have met people like this that are notable leaders and always seem to find themselves called or elected to lead others. Maybe this describes you!

I remember submitting the paper and sharing that I didn't feel I led anything during my first six months of pastoral ministry! I described that my leadership experience might resemble an inexperienced young cowboy that had been seated atop a very large intimidating and infuriated Brahma bull. The gate was thrown open, and with a snort from the bull, away I went. It could be best described as an uncontrolled flailing mass of human flesh trying desperately to hang on and stay in the saddle for the full eight seconds without being tossed into the sawdust and trampled underfoot. In that first year, I didn't feel like I led much of anything. I felt like I was always trying to keep my head above water without drowning. I think a lot of what I felt was attributed to the overwhelming feeling of unworthiness to be in the position I had been placed by God. I remember that I loved my people and prayed for guidance from God. I didn't give up and tried to always be positive in every situation. I did the things that were possible and left the rest for God to handle.

I worked hard to earn the trust of the congregation and the community. My first year in pastoral ministry yielded many opportunities to serve in some difficult situations. I know you have noticed several instances in the previous chapters where I have mentioned serving. To be a leader you must be willing to serve. To be an accomplished and successful leader, you will need to become a dedicated servant. That my friends is scriptural. During my first year as a full-time pastor in a small community of about three hundred people, I officiated a tremendous amount of funerals. There was a severe flood in the area, the hundred-year kind, and it severely affected the two local funeral parlors. We held many funerals in the churches and I was able to meet many people that I may not have met otherwise. During this time it was necessary to overcome some obstacles while meeting the needs of the people in the church and in the community. It was an honor to open our church to the family during a most difficult time for them.

Another trait of a good leader is one that is willing to make every necessary effort to serve someone in need. As a leader, you will always be leading people to God through many different pathways. It may be the pathway of being a counselor. It may be through visiting them in the hospital or their home. It may be when you speak to them in a store or on the street. Even though you may not initially see it this way, others see you as a leader in everything you do. Many times people will be willing to defer to you for comment or seek instruction because they recognize you as a leader.

I have a parishioner that has been a Fire Chief for many years, and he has given over fifty years of volunteer service to his community. He is well respected and has truly worked hard to earn the respect of the community. He has been privileged to serve in several elected positions in his county of residence. He made a statement that has been permanently imprinted into my mind and has found its way into this book. He stated, *"The effective leader is the one that leads in such a way that the followers are following without realizing the leader is leading."* An effective leader is one that will also be looking for leadership qualities in others. As you prepare to lead your congregation, you may very well find that you can relate to the description I offered in my class paper about being on the back of the bull. You can do it! God has your back! As you step into the role of leader, you will employ the attributes of loving your people and serving them as their pastor. You will feed them a diet rich in nutritious scripture while demonstrating the fruits of the Spirit in your life and spending time caring for them.

An appropriate recap for this chapter would be to suggest that one of the greatest attributes that you could employ as a leader is one that resembles the quality I described in my class instructor. Despite the fact you may feel like you are having difficulty, a leader with a genuine smile, a humble spirit, and the willingness to serve others and take the extra effort is something God can and will use. An effective leader will also be looking to bring others along with them while looking for others that also possess leadership qualities.

Another mentionable quality of a good pastor is that they know when it is time to leave. Your parishioners will better appreciate your visit when you keep your visit brief and appropriate to their condition. They do not feel well or they wouldn't be in the hospital.

CHAPTER 7

The Pastoral Comforter

It is no secret that people avoid uncomfortable situations. Being a pastor will surely place you right in the middle of some very uncomfortable situations in which you will be expected to be genuine, caring, and have all of the right words when needed. No worries there, right? I will touch on a few of these in this section. A key part of pastoral ministry will involve hospital and home visitation. I want to offer a few thoughts for you to consider about visiting people while they are in the hospital. It is important to consider the situation of those that are hospital confined. You must try to ascertain if there are any restrictions or special processes you must follow while visiting.

As I prepare this book, we are amid the COVID 19 pandemic of 2020 and the flu season is starting to ramp up in the area, so you must be careful if you are visiting someone with flu or anything contagious. You do not want take it home, or take it to another patient. If you have someone you are visiting that is immune-compromised due to chemotherapy you would not want to stop and visit Ms.

Jones that is there with the flu. Also, if you have someone that is immune-compromised and you are visiting them at home, you may want to visit them first thing in the day instead of last so you will decrease the chance of taking something to them during the visit.

Check with the hospitals you will be visiting and check with pastoral services. There you will find some good information regarding visitation restrictions. Some facilities may require you to take a class before you officially visit as a pastor. After the class, you may be issued an identification badge so staff will know who you are. Get to know the nurses and the people caring for your parishioners! They can be a wonderful asset to you as a pastor. You may find that as you nurture a relationship with the care providers, they may find you to have you visit or pray with someone on their unit that may be critically ill or without family. There are several potential scenarios that you may encounter, so I have listed a few of the more common ones you may face as you visit in the hospital.

An important part of hospital visitation is simply understanding the fact that these people are in the hospital. While hospitalized, patients may have been given medications that adversely affected them. They may not look or sound the same way they do on Sunday morning. They may be dressed in those wonderful and classy hospital gowns that are horrible when it comes to keeping ones privacy! Depending on what medications they have received, and how much they have received, you may arrive to find them in some awkward conditions. Sometimes your people will be undergoing procedures that require overnight preparation. On top of already being sick, anyone that has a bowel preparation is completely miserable. Sometimes you will realize immediately that they are not going to be able to sit for a visit and that you may need to come back later after the procedure has been completed. They may be in much better shape to enjoy a pastoral visit. You may arrive at the hospital and find Aunt Tessie may not have had time to put her false teeth in, or her makeup on, and she may be completely embarrassed that you have seen her this way. Your ability to act as if you are completely blind in these moments while commenting on the cars in the parking lot are not only welcomed but are treasured later as you help her maintain her dignity while she puts in her teeth. These are extremely important things to consider but the constant application of heaping doses of humbleness to help them maintain their dignity will go a long way with them in connecting with you as their pastor.

Another mentionable quality of a good pastor is that they know when it is time to leave. Your parishioners will better appreciate your visit when you keep your visit brief and appropriate to their condition. They do not feel well or they wouldn't be in the hospital. They know you love them and see you are demonstrating it by your visit. Most times they will try to be patient during your visit, but will appreciate it greatly when they see that you are showing consideration to them. If they want you to stay longer, they will tell you. It also seems to be an unwritten rule that preachers have the innate ability to arrive at the same time as the food tray or at the same time that nature calls. I always tell my parishioners I am a good pastor and a good pastor knows when it is time to go. I try not to stay any longer than ten to fifteen minutes unless asked otherwise. Don't forget to pray with them before you leave. They need it and may look forward to that prayer most of all. If it's semi-private room, you may consider offering prayer for their roommate as well. Be reminded that this isn't the time for a long prayer. Keep it simple and to the point. From their perspective, the best thing you can offer them is that prayer! I am also aware of their right to privacy and must stress here the need for keeping their details confidential. I have encountered a lot of parishioners that love to try to extract people's personal details from the pastor. Some of them are experts so you have to pay attention when you are asked about someone that you have visited, as some of these folks can download information from you with a hacker's skill.

While we are still talking about hospital visitation, let me address visits when the patients are critical and it is unknown at the time whether they will live. This can prove to be a very difficult and challenging scenario even for a seasoned minister. When you are visiting the critically ill you will have to follow your gut instincts. There will be times that you will arrive to find the family in shambles waiting for answers that will often bring bad news. In some of these cases, you will put on your best face and be there for whatever they need. You may just need to hold their hand and keep them from being alone. The same thing goes for the person in the bed. There are times they will want you to be their pastor but there will be times that they are sliding closer to God's side and will be comforted by the pastor being with them to hear their thoughts as well as having the close friend and confidant that will just hold their hand and steady them as they go home. In these cases, all bets are off and you will have to follow your gut and your heart.

I will never forget the first time I was allowed to be with a family during one of their most difficult times. I had been at my first full-time appointment less than a year when one of my parishioners was dealing with the passing of her mother. I didn't have an opportunity to meet her mother before this event and didn't know her, but, I did know her daughter and her husband. I went to visit them but sensed quickly that this lady was very close to going home. I did not feel that I could leave them. They seemed to understand and allowed me to spend many hours with them and seemed comforted that I was there. I met my parishioner's father while there. He was a very sweet man that deeply loved and adored his wife with everything he had in him. He did not leave her side and we did everything we could to keep him comfortable during that time. I remember praying with them and remember that they moved her from the ICU unit at the hospital to a hospice house across the street. They knew without a doubt that she was dying but the move to hospice was the confirmation of this. I met them there and was with them for a little while and then I went home. I wish I would have stayed because she passed a few hours later. In those cases, you don't leave the family. They need you even if they don't tell you. I gladly did the funeral for them. I visited the father on several occasions at his home. He attended another denomination but did attend one of my churches a few times. His daughter told me one day that he identified me as his pastor despite the fact he attended another church. This was one of those special moments when your heart swells and the tears fill your eyes. God has used you to touch someone completely unexpectedly. My wife and I are still close to this family and we love them dearly.

You may need to keep your leadership abreast of how you conduct your visitation and activities. You can explain to them about how you manage your visitation. It is a good idea to share with your leaders about how you develop your style so they know that you are on top of things and serious about visitation. One of the most common complaints that I have heard from churches about their pastor was that they did not visit enough. If you do not tell them, don't expect them to automatically know how much or how often you visit. It also heads off communication errors when you share with them how you consider their needs in regards to the spread of infection. They may not have thought of it, but after an explanation, will surely appreciate your forethought. No one will share the news of the ninety-nine that you visited, just the one hundredth that you didn't.

That being said, here is another tasty bit of knowledge you will surely love. You will not always know when or if they are in the hospital, but you will be expected to know! It is even more complicated today with Social Media. People tend to post their lives on social media, the good, the bad, the ugly. Some will expect you to keep up with them without them telling you anything that isn't on their page or timeline. It is hilarious how the same people who expect you to read their page will turn right around and fuss that you seem to spend too much time on social media. There are some that understand the difficulties that a pastor faces and are hesitant to add more to your duties. Maybe you have already experienced some of these situations or heard of them happening. Don't be surprised when you are about to take Monday off to spend with your family and have one of your sweet little members tell you that they are going to have surgery on Monday, a procedure that was scheduled a month ago, but you were never informed of it. Take a deep breath or six.

Let's talk a little more about home visitation. In some of my first classes as a lay minister, I had the privilege of taking an advanced preaching class that was five nights long. The pastor was a man my age, however, he had many years of pastoral experience behind him and I felt blessed to have the opportunity to learn under him. He told us one night during a class, in no uncertain terms, something that has stayed with me. He said, *"You can be the greatest preacher, singer, or teacher, but until you visit them in their home, they will not consider you their pastor."* He was absolutely spot on with his statement. When people see that you care enough to come and see them in their home, they will most certainly view you from a different perspective.

If you are visiting someone specifically, it is nice to give a courtesy call but if you are in the area, you may choose to drop in. I always apologize if I make a cold call to their home and tell them I completely understand if it is a bad time and offer to return at another time, if that is more convenient to them. I promise them that I will not be offended since I did not call ahead to get an okay. It shows respect to them and they will understand. As of this moment in time, I have never been turned away. When you go into their home, it is because they have accepted you, and invited you in. You will do yourself well by following their cue and doing as you are asked. They are about to make you their guest and you should feel privileged! I have been in houses that were so meticulously kept that I was uncomfortable walking past the door without removing my shoes. I have been in some homes that have been in such disarray that I wasn't able to see the floor! These will be your extremes and you will have to act accordingly. Just be gracious. It is with great respect that I enter a parishioner's home and I try my best to be respectful, and while in Rome, live as do the Romans. It seems to work very well.

There will be an occasion that you will learn that a parishioner or someone in the community is in dire need of help that they were reluctant to make known. I encountered this by accident once when dropping off a meal at a home. I was on my way home and I had agreed to drop off a hot meal from the local senior center at a home of a person that I had become acquainted within the community. This one was a cranky-tankerous tough individual and I mean that lovingly and respectfully. When I knocked on the door, I was not expecting an answer and was surprised to get an answer from the other side of the door. I was told to reach around through one of the front windows that were no longer there, and reach over and unlock the door. When I entered the house, there were no words that adequately described the picture. What I can say is that I observed a person lying in the rubble of the floor without shoes on. They were wearing a winter coat inside as it was about twenty degrees outside. There was no heat in the home. There was no water in the home. This person had been on the floor for over eighteen hours and unable to get up but was horrified I had witnessed their condition. That person pleaded with me to leave them and tried to make me believe they were ok. I had to lovingly disagree and that was difficult as I had no legal standing and was in their home by invitation. It took great patience and persistence to get them to agree this was an occasion to accept help. I had to call another individual to help me and it took ten minutes to move things away from the door to get the door open enough for the help to get inside the home. I was told later that I was the first person that had been allowed in that house for ten years. This visitation undoubtedly saved a human life. Being respectful and helping people maintain dignity can sometimes be very tough items to fit on the same plate but the results make it worth the effort.

Let's recap. You will be visiting people at their best as well as their worst. You will have to learn how to witness any type of potential scenario while maintaining a calm professional attitude. Take time to learn valuable information that will allow you to be most effective during your visits. Be humble and gracious, as well as patient, to the staff as well as the patient, and show respect. Be a good pastor and know when to leave. Use your resources. Listen to your heart and your gut, and be prepared for whatever presents to you. When you are welcomed into their home, you can go home and sleep well knowing they now consider you their pastor.

We love to see pictures of the shepherd holding the beautiful little spotless and precious white lamb. We also learn that the shepherd can get torn up trying to protect the sheep. In reality, the lambs can get into trouble but it is usually the adult sheep that are the headstrong ones and tend to get into deep trouble and jeopardize the health of the church and the shepherd.

CHAPTER 8

The Covenant Group

This could have been included in the self-care part but I did not because this is a different type of care that is specifically designed to address the pastor separate from the family. It is important for pastoral self-care and protection that you have someone to confide in and talk to. You will definitely need and benefit from having a spiritual buddy along the way.

You need someone on your level that you can talk openly and freely about the things you deal with as a pastor. It is also an opportunity to share and learn with each other. It should not be your spouse! Unless they are actively pastoring with you, it is not fair to your parishioners or your spouse to share confidential conversations in this way. For example; Brother Tom comes to you on Sunday morning and tells you that he wants to talk with you in your office after church. After church, he confides that he is being unfaithful to his wife. His wife Sarah, is your wife's best friend. There is no way you can go home and confide to your wife what Brother Tom has just shared with you. You will learn to appreciate the importance of the clergy covenant partner! It is a great asset to be able to meet with regularly to be able to discuss your feelings in a controlled and professional environment without worrying about having it repeated. I know you might be thinking about everything you have read up to this point and may be wondering how you might manage to have that much available time but you will be happy you did.

There are some cases where two or three pastors will form a clergy covenant group to have a support group for one another. They will meet a couple of times a month or less, usually over a meal. You really and truly need the space to be able to relax and also "vent" those difficult things that you have faced and stored away in your mind during your pastoral journey.

Don't feel badly when you realize that you are having feelings of being overloaded and stressed. The covenant pastor relationship has saved many a pastor from imploding as well as exploding. Sometimes in this relationship, the covenant pastor can help you realize that it may be time for you to take a day or two off, or even take a vacation. Make no mistake! You need this type of support! Simply put, it is very difficult for someone other than a minister or pastor to understand what you are going through. The mental respite you get during this time is priceless and these clergy covenants can help one in the relationship decompress and continue to be fruitful and productive. Once you have found your spiritual buddy, meet as regularly as you can swing it. Another benefit of the clergy covenant is the ability to share ideas and have discussions about a topic you love.

An important thing to mention here is that people will become very interested when they see a couple of pastors setting together having a good time. Be aware of the place you meet, as you will also learn that itching ears may become wagging tongues that take interest in seeing pastors talking in a corner. If possible, meet in a neutral area where you are less likely to have your conversations interrupted by well-meaning parishioners.

Finally, respect the covenant! One of the greatest potential problems pastors face is having someone in the group that cannot keep the confidentiality of the covenant. Forgive me, but there are few things more frustrating than a pastor that can't keep their mouth shut, breaking confidentiality. Used correctly, the covenant will allow you the freedom to decompress your mind and find comfort with other clergy members. It will allow you to discuss common struggles you are having in your church as well as your personal life. You can help each other with personal struggles and accountability regarding difficult situations. You can work through some simple as well as complex issues. You can also have someone that you can pray with on a direct spiritual level, and that is priceless!

I have a friend that currently is not serving as a pastor after suffering through two horrible pastoral experiences. I cannot tell you that a clergy covenant group would have made a difference but I can tell you for sure that it would have given him some support that he didn't have during his battles! I don't want to be a party pooper, but you already know or will learn that some church people can exhibit behavior that is less than Christian, especially when outside the church. Several members driving the "*Our Four and No More Self-Righteous Church Bus*" ran over my friend, and then they drug him along behind it for a bit. The devil will always take an open opportunity to attack. When he uses the sheep against the shepherd it is always a bad scenario. I am reminded of a few occasions that I would have rather been volunteered to trim the toenails of an aggravated bobcat in the back seat of a Toyota Prius than deal with some of the personalities that can occur in self-righteous "church people."

We love to see pictures of the shepherd holding the beautiful little spotless and precious white lamb. We also learn that the shepherd can get torn up trying to protect the sheep. In reality, the lambs can get into trouble but it is usually the adult sheep that are the headstrong ones and tend to get into deep trouble and jeopardize the health of the church and the shepherd. Sometimes during the process, the sheep can be injured past the point of being saved and the pastor can be fatally injured spiritually. This one is a short chapter but an important one. Please consider the importance of becoming part of a clergy covenant as you get established in your ministry. Your spiritual sanity will appreciate it.

I believe that the funeral is for the family and not the pastor.
If it comforts the family, then that is what is important.

CHAPTER 9

The Pastor as Funeral Officiant

The pastor will be summonsed, you can be sure, to be there for families when death calls. Hopefully, you will have had a chance to get to know the person or the family before the family needs you to officiate the funeral services. Maybe you had the opportunity to be with the family as their loved one departed, or was able to spend time with the deceased before their passing. If you have had the opportunity to get to know them and to pastor them before this event, it is a great honor to be present with them at the time of their passing. There are instances where you will be able to prepare the family before the passing and it can provide them great comfort. I have been privileged to be with many families during the moment of death. Many were these times when I was working in healthcare and before I was a pastor. The process of death can be something that will give you great comfort as a pastor. I am sure you may be questioning how death could provide comfort to the pastor. Let me try to explain. When you have spent time with people that have made their peace with God and know him and are actively seeking that meeting, it is a comfort to know that a promise of God is being fulfilled right before your very eyes. There are times that you can feel the presence of the Spirit of God in the room. There was one such occasion I experienced a sweet flowery smell in the room as the person was dying. It was unmistakable. There was more than one person present that witnessed this event and they knew something special had occurred during that death experience.

There will be times that you have the opportunity to do things for people that are very special moments in their lives, and yours. I once had the opportunity to baptize a lady in her hospital bed just a day or so before she went home to be with the Lord. She was in her early nineties and had never been baptized. It was such a comfort to her and was a comfort and a relief for her daughters. She lived within a rocks throw of the church but had not been able to attend in years, and it was a pure coincidence that I had happened to visit with her. God leads us to places that we may never have considered going. We just need to be willing and let him lead us where he will.

It has been my experience that the family looks to you as the pastor to lead them through the funeral service. You are looked at as the expert and you will talk with them about several things along the way as you help them prepare for the services ahead. Getting to know the funeral directors in your area will be a well-earned feather in your cap, as they will prove to be very good colleagues to have in your corner as you work together in ministry. Many times they know the families much better than you do and can help guide you about which family members are the best decision-makers or the ones best able to provide you the information you will need to plan the service. You will want to learn as much as you can about the deceased on your own, as well as asking family and friends for information about them. I have learned many things while in the wake to help me plan the service. Always remember it is their service, so they need to tell you what they want people to hear during the service. I am always very eager to try and accommodate requests for the funeral. I have had many that included family and friends speaking during the time of remembrance. It really helped me out tremendously when they took part in the service.

When I begin the message part of the service, I am considerate of a couple of things. First, is that person saved or not? We must be very careful because we do not have the ability as pastors to preach anyone into Heaven or out of Hell after death. When the person is saved, the funeral is much easier to share with family about the promises of God that their loved one is enjoying at that very moment; but, if the person was not, we must be considerate to acknowledge that they are in the hands of a just God. I always include the message of salvation during the service but I always run that by the family. I have never been turned down to date and am frequently told after the service that it was a comfort to a family that it was being given during the sermon.

I was called once by a funeral director to do a funeral for someone that left the area over sixty years ago and was returned to the area to be buried. She had made those wishes clear to her family. The family wanted a service but knew no one in the area. I am not sure that they had ever set foot in the community until her death. She lived her life six hundred miles away but wanted to come back to her hometown to be interred into hometown soil. I was honored to be called upon to help but found it a very difficult situation. The family did not want any songs. They didn't know any hymns and said that their mother was not religious and there was no indication she had any relationship with God. They had no memories that they wanted to be shared and no one wanted to speak or say anything. I didn't want to have a five-minute funeral and it took some doing to perform a reasonable service. Thankfully, there was a distant relative that was one of my parishioners, and that helped me out. Praying slowly and with much thought was a great help. It was a very basic service with a very generic scripture read. We were able to make the family comfortable and meet the wishes of the departed to get her buried on native soil. After the funeral, the director told me that they didn't exactly know what to do with this particular case, but, after working with me in the past, thought that if anyone could make it work, I was their choice. I went back home that day mentally tired but inspired. I learned a lot that day and I have that sermon locked away just in case I am called on another day in a similar situation.

When I was a very young and fledgling minister, I purchased a book that was a pastor resource book. It contained funeral service and wedding service outlines that you could adjust to your needs. It offered many selections for an array of situations and I still have it in my library all these years later. Today, you can easily find a funeral outline on the internet with just a few clicks of your mouse. Some denominations also have outlines available that you could preview. I officiated my first funeral when I was in my twenties, and my pastor at the time was very helpful to me in preparing me for how to handle the service. I will offer you the same information that was given to me. I found it invaluable and have always taken it to heart. Keep to the point and under thirty minutes if possible. Unless this is someone that is having a special service performed by the military, a fraternal lodge or an EMS/Fire/Police service, you should have them ready to leave for the cemetery in thirty minutes. By this time the family is running on reserve because they are worn out. They are ready to get this part over and begin their closure. There are cases when the officiating pastor is from a very small church and they are thrilled to preach to a room full of people. This situation can become an irresistible temptation to wax long, and be a pain to the family. Further, when you get to the cemetery you should be brief but respectful. Leaving the loved one at the cemetery can be challenging, and how you handle the graveside part of the service can be instrumental in their closure.

My usual services have generally included one to three songs that are spaced out through the service based upon what the family desires. My service usually begins with a welcoming and opening prayer, followed by a song. After the song there are the opening comments, reading of the obituary, a time of remembrance of their life. Usually, a song follows. Sometimes there will be more than one minister for the funeral service. If I am their pastor at the time of the death, unless asked to make other arrangements, I do the message part of the service and the other minister will do the opening part of the service. After the message, there may be a song and then a closing prayer. At this point, the funeral service is ready to take the next step. HINT: It is a good idea to type up and print multiple copies of the service outline to give to the funeral director. It saves time and makes things run smoother as they can follow along with the service and know when to be present. Here is a rough and simple outline of a very basic funeral service.

- Welcome and Opening Prayer
- Song
- Reading of the Obituary
- Opening remarks and review of life of deceased
- Offer opportunity for those that want to speak
- Song
- The Pastoral Message
- Song
- Closing Prayer.
- Dismiss to Cemetery

Arrival Cemetery

- Scripture Reading
- Prayer
- Dismissal

I want to address something here that I have encountered, and, at times, have struggled with. There will be times you will be offered an honorarium for your services at funerals, or weddings. Each person needs to make their own decision on how they may choose to accept or refuse to accept this offering. I have discussed this on several occasions with my colleagues and I have been given feedback from them that has helped me tremendously. When someone is a member of my congregation, I feel I owe them that courtesy to take care of them at their time of need without a thought of an honorarium. I have thought similarly for weddings of couples that are members of the church. I will go into the wedding aspect in the next chapter. I have really had times that I stressed over being offered an honorarium for service.

I had the opportunity to officiate a funeral for a relative of one of my church families. They were fantastic people and I quickly agreed to do the funeral. During the interview of the family, I commented that I knew a person about thirty-five years ago with the same last name and asked if it could be a relative. As it turned out, that just happened to be the person I was speaking to and the deceased was his mother! I was speechless. I was a mere nineteen years old at the time and he wasn't much older. This family lived fifty miles from where I grew up and the chances we would meet on this path thirty-five years later was very unusual, to say the least. The funeral went very well and our church hosted a meal for the family after the interment. After the dinner, this fellow came to me and offered me an honorarium. I didn't feel I could take it. It was such an honor to have this opportunity to serve them and I graciously made my thoughts known to him. He told me that I blessed their family and they wanted to bless me in turn. I asked them if they would consider taking that honorarium and donating it to the church in his mother's honor. That honorarium was a very substantial donation to the church. I was floored at their generosity. I actually performed two more funerals for this family while pastor there.

There was another situation that I was called on to perform a funeral for a lady that I did not know. Her sister attended one of my churches, so once again, I was happy to comply with her request. It was a very basic and simple funeral and once it was over, the sister came to me and offered me an honorarium. Once again I was feeling great trepidation about accepting the honorarium. I hugged her and told her that I was honored she asked me to do the funeral for her sister and that her thanks and hug was more than enough honorarium for me. She hugged me very hard and when she stepped back her eyes were wet with tears. She told me that her sister had nothing and that she was struggling to make the funeral payment. She told me that I must have had that sense about me to feel that because she had prayed hard that she needed to give me something for the funeral but didn't know where that would come from. I sensed that it came from her own pocket. I didn't see what the amount was but was completely at peace with my choices.

My best advice for you would be to follow your heart about it. I have been extremely blessed by some of the families I have served and had the peace of mind that they were doing it out of love and respect instead of out of a feeling that it was an obligation. As pastors, we know we are in ministry for the outcome and not the income. But, that being said, we must also understand that sometimes God will use people to bless us along the way and we should not do something in a way that prevents God from blessing us.

One final note before ending this chapter. You may be called upon to officiate a funeral in a church that you are not the current pastor. If you are asked by a family to go to another church location to officiate a funeral, ask the family if they have contacted the current pastor to be sure that the pastor is good with it. It is important to respect the other pastor's position. Sometimes things get dropped in the shuffle with a family that is preparing to attend to a loved one's last requests and notifying the pastor can be overlooked by family. It is conceivable the family may not have had to arrange a funeral before this one and may assume it to be the job of the funeral director to notify the pastor. A simple phone call to the hosting pastor can alleviate issues for the future and it demonstrates your professional character. In a perfect scenario, the pastor of the hosting church will call you and let you know that you will be welcomed to handle the funeral.

You may encounter a scenario when someone dies that you do not know, however, the family identifies your church as being their home church. I encountered this situation, having been called to the home at the hour after death to comfort and pray with the family, even before the deceased was taken from the home. I was happy to meet and pray with the family in their hour of need. I was asked by the spouse if I would be willing to officiate the funeral. I was happy to comply even though I did not know them. I knew some of their relatives, who were active members of the church. The next day I learned through a third party, that another pastor from a different church had invited himself to handle the funeral. I expect he was aware that they identified with my church. There are more details regarding the situation which would make this easier to understand, however, I am intentionally omitting it for the sake of professionalism. I attended the funeral wearing attire that identified me as a pastor so people knowing that the family identified with our church would also know that our church was represented in honor of the passing. I was further surprised to learn this pastor, after inviting himself to officiate, had invited a second pastor to officiate with him. Again, there is more information intentionally omitted. I did not allow it to affect me for a couple of reasons. I believe that the funeral is for the family and not the pastor. If it comforts the family, then that is what is important. Do not get your feathers ruffled if this happens to you. Be gracious and remember it is about what the family needs. It will be a blessing to you later. You may have to have a conversation with the pastor if the behavior becomes a future trend. Most times, it is simply a big-hearted pastor with wonderful intentions. That is commendable as they only want to do the right thing and may have forgotten that the family had church affiliation, especially if the family does not regularly attend. This scenario is more common than you think. Some families will go years and never attend your church, but in their minds, are still a part of the church. Occasionally, you will run into a pastor that may not like your denomination or any denomination that is not theirs, and may feel threatened by other pastors. Yes, they exist and can occasionally be a thorn in your flesh. As long as you act in the best interest of the family, you will be fine.

Couples are spending exorbitant amounts of money that they do not have, on the wedding of a lifetime, which, will only last a few hours. They are pinching pennies when it comes to investing in the solid foundation that they will need to begin their marital journey on a strong footing.

CHAPTER 10

The Pastor and the Nuptials

My first comment about weddings is to tell you to be sure that you understand and follow all legal processes and meet the requirements to perform weddings in your state! Experiences will vary but I can offer you information that you can use. You can read it and use the information as you can. I offer this as my opinion only, based on my own experiences.

Counseling. Any couple that calls on you to perform a wedding for them should undergo premarital counseling! This is especially important if this is their first marriage. I realize that the comment "*first marriage*" may create some anxiety for some of you, but sadly, divorce happens. There are many young men and women that have been married with little to no counseling beforehand and no idea of what it was going to be like being married. Many of those had no church experience and their lives an unorganized chaotic mess that ended much like a plane being flown with no one at the controls. I understand this very well since I was one of those young people and experienced all of the pain that goes along with the horrible crash that inevitably follows. I am in my mid-fifties now and married happily for over thirty years. There is healing, there is grace and I believe that there is forgiveness. Remember, as a pastor you are performing the ritual of Christian marriage that is rooted in biblical principles.

There are online assessment tools available, and based on the couple›s answers, will provide information that will allow them to become aware of their potential strengths and weaknesses that they will face as a married couple. It can also identify areas where they may face challenges or need more help.

I recently took a class to become a facilitator for just such a course. I am adding this with the permission of the owners. SYMBIS, which stands for *"Save Your Marriage Before It Starts,"* is a wonderful option for those seeking marriage. Doctors Les and Leslie Parrott have put together a wonderful program that enables one to become a certified facilitator. This information can be found at www.symbis.com. The couple can take the assessment and the data will populate based on their answers and be available to you as the facilitator. You will receive the data and be able to use the information to discuss with the couple when you meet with them. Don't be afraid to meet with them more than once! Don't be afraid to ask the hard questions!

Marriage is a process that works only if both parties take it seriously and with total commitment. If couples are serious about being married, it is worth working with them and doing it right. If they aren't willing to commit to that type of counseling and become involved in the process that can help them identify and work through areas that might cause them problems later, you might consider passing on the wedding. If your couple clears the previous hurdle, talk to them about how they understand marriage from the biblical perspective. You must ascertain this before you go farther with them. You are going to ask God to bless this union. If they are not interested in *"hearing the religious stuff,"* you should be worried and consider referral to another officiant that is non-religiously affiliated. Premarital counseling can actually be enjoyable. You will be surprised at some of the answers you will hear in pre-marital counseling sessions, but try not to let that show on your face. You can be assured that you might hear some answers you never saw coming! You will be intrigued by some of the answers that you get to the questions you ask. A lot of who we are and how we believe is based upon those that influenced us in life.

Here is a good example of a fictional story to help you see this more clearly. A young couple had been married about a month. As they sat down for dinner, the husband looked at the beautiful roast that was on the table and posed a question to his wife. *"Why did you cut both ends off of the roast when you put it in the pan to cook?"* His wife looked at him and shrugged her shoulders and answered. *"That's the way mom does it."* Intrigued by this answer, the husband inquires further as to why her mother cut the ends off of the roast, and receives the answer from the wife that she really didn't know. The following day the newlyweds were visiting her parents. She asked her mother during the visit why she cut both ends off of the roast before putting it in the pan to cook. Her mother looked at her thoughtfully for a moment and answered. *"That's the way my mother did it."* When asked why grandma did this, mom couldn't answer.

Grandma was still living so mother picks up the phone and calls grandma up. She says *"Mom, why did you always cut the ends off of the roast before you placed it in the pan to cook?"* Grandma laughs on the other end of the phone. She answered, *"Honey, we were so poor, it was years before I could afford a pan big enough to cook a whole roast. I had to cut the ends off to make it fit!"* We repeat what we have observed. People do things for many reasons. Some reasons may not turn out to be the wisest or best reasons, but it may be all they know.

It can be embarrassing to find that your view on something is based on here-say or hand me down information that was never explained or understood. That's enough on this.

In this region, there is an increasing number of couples that are choosing to be married in locations other than the church. There are many different wedding venues and options available in the current era. I am aware of one that offers a wedding experience on a working farm, and another locally available option that offers a wedding in a specially built barn. Couples are spending exorbitant amounts of money that they do not have, on the wedding of a lifetime, which, will only last a few hours. They are pinching pennies when it comes to investing in the solid foundation that they will need to begin their marital journey on a strong footing. Another important thing to mention here. Before you perform a ceremony, be sure to put your eyes on, and preferably have in your hand, the marriage license! I have personally decided that I will not be a part of a sideshow that is more about the wedding experience than the wedding commitment. If the couple is committed to the marriage,

I will do everything I can for them before the marriage and remind them that I am available after the marriage too. For those just looking for marriage but not willing to commit to the required counseling and not seeking a spiritual commitment, there are licensed wedding officiants available that can help them out and I am happy to let them take care of it, especially, if the couple isn't serious about their commitment.

Let me refer once again to something from earlier. Honorarium. If you are performing the ceremony for a couple that is spending six thousand dollars on the wedding location, a thousand dollars on the booze, and another five hundred on the dee-jay for the after-party and then another thousand on the food, you should not be hesitant to accept an honorarium for your time and travel. One last tip, be sure you find out if you are required, as the officiant, to file the signed marriage license after the marriage. Become very familiar with the laws and regulations regarding marriage in your state. I like personally to deliver the signed license back to the courthouse for my own peace of mind.

Let's say that all has gone well in the above paragraphs and the couple is now married and living in bliss, keep in touch with them and encourage them. If they have questions, be available to them and be ready to provide help to them, if necessary.

Instead of listening to learn and be informed, we are busy forming our response before we completely hear the story. We must be patient and listen with the intent as to what is being said to us. Listen to what is being said to you!

CHAPTER 11

The Pastor as Counsellor

There will instances whereby you will be called upon to give some type of pastoral counseling. By design, you will be considered as someone who is a trustworthy facilitator of communication. As you go forward in ministry, I pray you will be looked upon as a figure of trust and integrity. It goes without saying that you most assuredly will work very hard to attain this honor. It is here that your attention to maintaining confidentiality is paramount. Most times you will find that you are able to handle most requests for counseling very easily and appropriately and without incident, but there are a few things you may want to consider along the way. Are you a good listener? Being a good pastoral counselor requires you to be a good listener to what people are telling you. It also means that you are trying to be aware of the nonverbal cues that people will be showing, cues that will give insight into what is concerning them. There is one pitfall that is common during counseling. It is listening while looking for the opportunity to give your answer. Instead of listening to learn and be informed, we are busy forming our response before we completely hear the story. We must be patient and listen with the intent as to what is being said to us. Listen to what is being said to you! There is nothing wrong with repeating back what you hear so you can be sure you got it right. Also, if you are unsure, clarify what is being requested or what the conversation is about. You may be being asked to lend an ear to allow someone to vent their problems. They may not want a response and only need to get it off their chest. You will become a much better listener if you understand what you need to be listening for.

There are some people you will encounter that will come to you and want to talk about a particular issue and then go off on a tirade for the next ten minutes about something completely different. This can be confusing and it takes being able to carefully listen to get to the place that you are able to see what is really ailing or bothering the individual. Once again, there are times you may have to clarify the parameters of the meeting to understand what is occurring.

One more important little statement needs to be added. Protect yourself! Do not meet with individuals behind closed doors alone! If you are having a meeting with someone, do it in an area that is open to the public or with your spouse or another person. It is also a good idea not to meet someone of the opposite sex without another individual present. Never counsel a minor child without the presence of a parent or a related adult. If I am being asked to counsel a female I will take my wife along. She does not have to be in the middle of the conversation but she is close enough to be an overseer that all things are in order. Protect yourself and your reputation at all costs, as the devil would like nothing better than to take a cheap shot at you while you are trying to be of assistance. This is a good place to suggest you consider obtaining and having in place a malpractice policy. You can ask the church if you are covered by their malpractice insurance, but do not hesitate to obtain your own.

Marital counseling:

You may be called upon to work with couples having marital issues. The couple may be under a load of stress before they bring you into the equation. By this time tensions could be very high and make the situation even more difficult for you as you get involved. Proceed with caution! Listen very carefully to what they are telling you verbally and non-verbally so you may gain as much understanding by seeing their body language or what it appears they are not telling you. One of the most important clues to look for is if the problem is much different than something spiritual. If their problems seems to be other than spiritual issues you will need to be prepared to send them for professional counseling. Furthermore, when someone that has been married for twenty years comes to you with a history of not attending church and gives you a laundry list of issues they are fighting over, and that fighting began a year after their marriage, pastors are usually no match for this type of counseling nightmare. Unless one has a specific degree and experience in that area, this is the time to send them to the professional, as you are likely to make things worse. Be prepared to help them find a professional counselor as it is the right thing to do.

If it seems to be a reasonable counseling challenge that I believe I am capable of handling. I still listen for possible safety concerns to assure that during this time of distress that there are no other unhealthy things occurring in the marriage. I will try to help them if the problem seems to have a reasonably simple solution. It could be something as easy as fighting over which parent they go have their Sunday dinner. If you encounter a situation that you don't think two or three meetings with them can get them going in the right direction, it is time to send them to the professionals. I suggest talking with each one separately to hear what each identifies as the issue and then bring them in together, with the understanding that you will share with them what each identifies as their issues. Be aware of cues of toxic matters that bringing them together would promote a potentially violent response. Once again, if you discern that this is a possibility, it may be best to refer this couple to a professional level of counseling.

Faith Related Issues:

Common issues you will deal with are related to people struggling with their faith. These conversations require patience and compassion. When people are coming to you with faith problems they are allowing themselves to be very vulnerable to your expertise. They deserve your full attention and compassion. Do not schedule someone for a conversation about their faith if you cannot give one hundred percent of your attention. Do not answer phones or texts during this time! Turn off the cell! As they describe their issue, I encourage you to listen to them very carefully. You must handle them where THEY are spiritually and not where YOU are spiritually.

One piece of advice that someone struggling with faith issues does not want to hear is that they just need to pray about it. I remember how this felt from personal experiences in my younger years. I remember going to some pastoral figures over a couple of super significant issues that I was struggling with. I was in my late twenties and the issues were causing me to lose peace of mind regarding my faith and position with the church. I spoke with two pastors during this event. The first one told me to "just pray about it." Well…duh…I am smart enough to pray and had prayed plenty. I did pray and I didn't get an answer so now I am here talking with you! The second pastor I spoke with was a complete waste of my time and his. I carefully explained to him about the issue and why I was seeking counsel from another pastor over this particularly troubling spiritual event. He kind of mumbled a little and nodded after each sentence, all the while, he was looking over the top of my head into space. At the end of my explanation of the issue, he looked at his watch and said, "Well, let's just let God be God." No one that has a faith issue should face those types of answers. There are times, though, that we will not have the answer to situations that we encounter. There is no shame if you are unable to provide the answer someone is seeking. It will be a help to them if you genuinely look them in the eye, take their hand, and tell them that you don't have the answer but, you do understand how difficult it is for them. Offer to pray with them for an answer and offer to help them find one. Sometimes that is the best you can do but this response does show love and it protects their integrity and demonstrates that their concern is real and important to you.

Whatever issue you may face with counseling people about their faith, it is important that you follow scripture and keep personal feelings out of the equation. I have had more than a few encounters that I had to smile and bite my lip over issues related to faith. If you aren't careful, people will really try to stretch the gospel way out of context. I assisted a very nice couple a few years ago. They had both lost their spouse many years earlier and were considering a possible future together. They were both having a hard time financially and decided to move into the same home. Eventually, each of them came to me to have a discussion about living together. Neither knew that I had previously talked with the other one. I was asked if it was permissible by God for that other person to live in the home. I began to ask some questions about just how that person would be living in the home. I asked if that person was paying rent to live there. I asked if there was any type of "benefits" in the arrangement. I advised that any physical activity that resembled marital behavior should be avoided. I also advised that however, they chose to live they should not allow it to keep them from being faithful to church and to God. I was told that they were married in their hearts and God knew their hearts. I suggested that although that might even be true, the law viewed it a bit different and it was definitely going to be a witness killer. There is much more to this story that is pertinent, but I'll leave it there. I am mentioning it because it refers to the part about keeping comments on a scriptural level. I took some heat from some self-righteous and nosey church people that didn't think they should be allowed to attend church. I stood firm on the fact that these people would absolutely be welcomed in the church and affirmed that we had plenty of room at our altar for all types of sinners and this even included the galloping gossipers and the nosey Nellies. End of discussion. The couple married within a year and still attend church.

Professional Individuals:

You may learn that you have someone in your church that is a professional. I am referring to those types that are a firefighter, paramedic, EMT, police officer, healthcare provider, attorney, or military soldier. These are people that are normally operating under a lot of stress and may be carrying heavy burdens before reaching out for your help. You will learn that they work daily with situations that are both heartbreaking and frustrating. They are cut from a different cloth than most and are wired with a very high tolerance for the issues that they face in their lives. I have always believed that these types of people are working in a calling much like a ministerial calling. Not just anyone can handle the situations that these people are expected to handle on a daily basis. These ladies and gentlemen have witnessed more tragedy in a week than most people see in a lifetime.

It is important that you are prepared for anything if you counsel with them. Be ready to hear anything! It is a real honor to be able to sit with these people in their time of distress or need, and sometimes, the simple description of what is bothering them may make you very uneasy in your seat. It is extremely difficult for them to ask for help because they are always the ones providing it. You may even be called upon to counsel a group of them such as firefighters after a particularly bad call and it is a wonderful asset if you happen to have a background in some of these fields. This group of workers is also a class of people that may require referral to a professional counselor; but, be aware that some, such as police officers, are hesitant to get help because it could negatively affect their career. Tread carefully here.

When I was an EMS provider, I lived by two *"Golden Rules."* The first rule was that people will die on you. The second rule was that no matter how smart you are or how good you were at your job, sometimes, you were powerless to change rule number one. I was once called upon to meet with a group of firefighters and 911 Communicators after a fire in a local community took the life of a child. It had been a very hard time for them and I had little knowledge of the event before being called upon to meet with them. During the meeting, I was able to take them completely through the call from the time of the initial call into the 911 Center and walk them through every moment of the details of the call in its entirety. Although it could not change the outcome of the event and did not ease the pain, it allowed each person to revisit the event in a thorough and controlled manner. This allowed them to compare notes and stories and hear from each other about how they were involved in, and affected by the call. In the end they were able to see that they really had done everything humanly possible in their response and nothing was left out. Although their hurt was still there, they were able to conclude that they had truly given their best effort and working together, they could find their way to some closure even though they could not save the child. This counseling session helped those professionals be able to move forward and be ready to answer the next emergency.

This session helped me affirm my sense that I was called to help this special family of providers.

In review, regardless of the type of situation, you are asked to counsel, keep in mind the dynamics of each situation as well as your own reputation. Protect yourself and your church and do not place yourself at unnecessary risk. Be a good listener and give your full attention to the details. Be sure you understand what is being asked of you. Know your limits and don't be afraid to refer to professional counselors. Keep your personal opinions out of the situation and be careful about how you answer even if they ask for your opinion. Always be compassionate and let them know you are concerned about them and care for them even when you do not have the answer they seek. Keep it in line with scripture and do not be afraid to stand your ground if needed. And keep confidential matters confidential!

Your spouse is your most dependable partner in ministry other than God, and they are the shoulder upon which you can lean and safely find rest.

94

CHAPTER 12

Pastoral Spouse

This chapter is going to speak to the wonderful person that has your back when the going is good, and also continues to have your back when it could be going better! Your spouse has many expectations being placed on them during this time. They are trying to support you while trying to get to know a new church family too. Your spouse is your most dependable partner in ministry other than God, and they are the shoulder upon which you can lean and safely find rest. They are your other half, or in some cases, your better half! It can be understandably harder for the spouse than it is for the pastor and it is important that you regard cautiously and carefully their place in this ministry paradigm. It was discussed earlier in the work about the importance of including them in the many decisions pertaining to entering the ministry. It was even discussed that it can be best to avoid including them in some situations whereby their knowledge of some information may not be the best choice. You will soon realize the level of importance and attention that you will place upon looking out for your spouse and protecting them as you are getting settled into your ministry.

Going into a new relationship with a church family will definitely have its stresses. You will most certainly hear all sorts of stories from other pastors and people about your church. I advise you to smile, thank them, and take it with a grain of salt as you let it go in one ear and out the other because there is always two sides to a coin. It is very reasonable and expected for you to feel some hesitation during this time but each church has its own personality. It is noteworthy to mention that all churches have good traits and that all churches have traits that could be better. Some churches are very loving by nature and they will quickly and completely embrace you and your family. There will be some churches that may come across as a bit more hesitant for reasons that will not initially be known to you. This is something that may be a day to day relationship until you both get to know the congregation and the congregation gets to know you. You will hear horror stories where the pastor was accepted but there was an issue reported that the spouse was not treated very well. I have heard similar stories where the church families loved the spouse but didn't relate well to the pastor. My wife and I have had very positive experiences with our churches and the families we have served. They have loved my wife as much as they have loved me and it has made life so much easier for us. Both of you will expend a good amount of effort trying to put the congregation at ease as you begin to take up your duties as pastor. Love your people! Let God reveal things in His time. I believe that applying this process is why we have had very positive results in our ministry.

It is important to understand that not only did your life change when you became a pastor but, so did your spouses. Most spouses will tell you they did not realize just how much the day to day life of a pastor consumes both pastor and spouse. There will be many meetings, visitations, phone calls, and people showing up at the door at all hours of the day and night. Although you try to keep reasonable hours and availability, there will be some that will seek out the pastor regardless of the hour when trouble arises. There will be members of the community that has not darkened a church door in decades but will come calling and knocking when something in the family dynamics goes wrong. Life for the pastoral spouse can be very overwhelming trying to retain balance during such trials.

I love taking my wife along on visitations whenever possible. It helps her develop healthy relationships with the congregants as well as providing welcomed assistance in remembering things after we leave, or after we have made a few visits. She benefits by being aware of things in the bigger picture that may be just around the corner such as a pending death or funeral. As you are getting acclimated to your new environment, be mindful that your spouse doesn't try to take on too many projects! You may have one of those motivated superstar spouses that have the tendency to take off like a whirlwind and get things done super-fast and in a hurry. I would advise a slower approach and takeoff until you get to know the mannerisms and expectations of your people a little better. What might be considered self-motivated in one place may be viewed as intrusive and overstepping in another and the last thing you want to do is ruffle their feathers unnecessarily or prematurely. There may be times that you have to protect your spouse from being assigned too many tasks because there are some church members that will want to volunteer your spouse for everything coming down the trail. This can prove to be a very stressful thing for both of you.

Be supportive of one another and have many discussions about how you will work together in ministry. It is imperative that you work as a cohesive team! My wife was never someone who enjoyed being in the middle of a crowd. She was not the type of person you would expect to find at the front door greeting people or volunteering to chair a church project.

She was, however, quick to learn that her presence and involvement was not only very welcome, but she found that she was helpful to me in many other ways. Her presence was extremely helpful on visitations and meetings or gatherings that represented our churches. I always appreciated that she always tried to be right there with me during these events.

Protect each other! You should have a frank and open discussion about how people may try and use the spouse as a pathway to gain different forms of information. It is difficult to have to admit that this happens, however, sadly it is an issue that is more common than anyone would like to admit. It is a well-known fact that humans are very nosey by their nature and church people can take nosey to new levels. There are people out there that will try their very best to align themselves with the pastoral spouse for the purpose of gaining as much information as possible for themselves or other people in the congregation. This information may not always be used for good intentions and may eventually be twisted around and used later for less than holy purposes.

The same applies to the pastor too! There are those that will try to do the same thing to you! They will try to obtain information from you that could be used later to manipulate you or throw you under the bus.

There is one more important item that needs to be mentioned. How thick is your skin? How thick is the skin of your spouse? Is either of you easily upset by those with opinions? I want to say this carefully, lovingly, and with respect, but some church folk can be downright unreasonable and impossible to please and their demeanor can get downright nasty! Some will complain your spouse is not doing enough. Some will complain that the spouse is doing too much. There will be complaints that the people should get to see the spouse more and some will complain that the spouse is around too much. There may be complaints the spouse shops too much, wears too much jewelry, too much makeup, or always seems to have a new outfit and where did that money come from?

Are you beginning to understand what I am speaking about? One of the reasons this needs to be mentioned is that on good days these personalities can be easily shrugged off, but on a difficult day, or when two or three bad days come together to be a week, it can become very overwhelming when added to the rest of your worries. Be prepared for the chattering tongues and their toxins. Although this group of people usually make up less than one percent of the congregation, they may make more noise than an angry mule kicking its way out of a tin barn stall and involve up to ninety percent of your aggravation. Love your people, but do not open yourself to unnecessary problems!

There are some of you that are reading this and are

not married, and in no hurry to get married. Marriage may not even be a consideration for you at the moment. Just a suggestion for you. It could prove beneficial to plan on addressing this subject in the earliest part of your interactions with your potential church members, as they undoubtedly will be interested in learning all about you and your family. Although it could be challenging, be courteous to lay some groundwork for them to understand and follow, if there is some pertinent history regarding your marital status. If you have lost a spouse or are divorced, it may be easier for you to share this in the initial steps so that it isn't an uncomfortable issue that comes up later on. If you are happy with the single life, you might want to let them know about that too, or the local congregation matchmaker may just target you for their next success story! Also, remember that unanswered questions in the minds of church people can potentially lead to the wagging tongue syndrome and the distorting of details, or the manufacturing of their own information to suit their taste.

Let's review this chapter. Your spouse is a wonderful partner for the journey of ministry that you are now embarking upon. It is important to look out for the overall safety and wellbeing of your spouse during the initial phase of ministry as you both seek to find your groove. Be particularly aware of how your relationships are developing with your congregation and be wary of anyone that seems to be overly or unnecessarily interested in your business. Don't let your spouse take on too many roles, as well as not letting them become the church's personal work mule. Unmarried folks. Honesty and openness in the beginning, may avoid future miscommunication and hard feelings later.

You will encounter situations in which people will expect you to climb a mountain in the dark, and then wrestle a bear, to complete a task that they are unwilling to cross the street on a sunny day to do themselves.

CHAPTER 13

Principles of Problematic & Peculiar Nature: Things That Go "Bump" in the Church

The event that I am choosing to share with you occurred during a rather normal day in my life. The day seemed to be proceeding at its usual pace. I want to insert a comment here, but what my wife and I considered normal, others might choose to describe as relatively well-controlled and robust states of chaos. On this day, I had a desk completely full of various ongoing issues in various stages of completion, but, had taken a brief respite and was sitting in my recliner resting and studying over some material for an upcoming sermon. I had taken the opportunity to enjoy an afternoon cup of coffee. My phone rang during the afternoon hours. It wasn't unusual for my phone to ring, however, the topic of conversation and the presumption of the person involved was one of those more memorable conversations that I have never forgotten and I admit that I was miffed and stunned at the conclusion of it.

Upon answering the phone, I was greeted by a voice that I recognized immediately. It was not unusual to receive a call from this person so there was no cause for concern on my part. As the call progressed I began to notice I was having greater difficulty finding the usual joy I normally experienced when we spoke by phone. I hung up the phone at the end of the call and replayed the entire conversation back in my head before deciding if I had indeed heard what I thought heard. I was beginning to think I had nodded off in the chair and the whole thing was just a dream. I decided that I was indeed awake and this was not a dream. The call went something like this. It began in a normal way and then started to revolve around the health and wellbeing of one of the aged parishioners who was a regular member of the church. It was a pertinent topic of concern and it was no secret that health difficulties had plagued this person terribly and resulted in their not being able to physically attend church services. There had been a couple of weeks that had passed since this person was last able to be in attendance. Unbeknown to this caller, I had been in contact with this member on a couple of recent occasions but did not feel it was necessary to talk about it at the moment.

As the conversation continued, the caller's intention became clear. It was suggested that someone needed to go see this person and personally check on them. Then the conversation quickly turned into the directive that I should be the one to come and make the visit to determine this person's wellbeing. After all, this is the pastor's job, right? This actually sounds like a reasonable request, right? Well, let me add more information to this recipe. The caller knew I was at my home and was very aware of my personally scheduled obligations. The caller was also very well aware that the other person's medical issues had been ongoing for quite some time. A couple of significant issues were becoming immediately obvious with this request. The first problem was that the one that was calling me on the phone just happened to live within eyesight of the person they were calling me about! There was no deep ravine, chasm, river, or great distance involved. A vehicle was not even required for them to go visit. The distance from one front porch to the other was mere yards apart. A good golfer could close the distance from the tee with one stroke of their driver. The one calling for this visitation was retired and had no physical or social issues that precluded them from visiting this church member just as easily as anyone else. That's every Christian's duty, right? There were no issues that prevented them from simply walking over to the home and knocking on the door.

Now, I will add the second issue into this recipe. It was very clear their intention was that I needed to drop everything that I was doing at that moment and go and make the visit. Just so you understand that I was not being contrary and that my state of frustration was justified, it is a hundred-mile round trip for me to do the requested visitation. There was even an inferred expectation that I should make the trip, drive all the way back home, and call and give a report of what I learned. Actually, I was invited to stop by if I wanted to stop in after the visit. That requested visitation did not happen, and the neighbor did not walk across the street either.

It can be an uncomfortable and embarrassing scenario to admit that an individual, or, group of individuals in a church congregation would hold membership for the simple and sole purpose of running the show their own way or are present simply to compromise congregational integrity. That being stated, let us look at some issues and situations that may become visible in the future of the new pastor. There are pastors that have received many spiritual injuries during their journey, and still, retain the scars inflicted by issues that have arisen when church members have wielded their membership in the form of a weapon. These are memories that pastors would like to forget. It is hard to believe that people would act this way and still testify and proclaim the greatness of our God. Don't kid yourself, they are out there and you will probably get introduced to a few.

As you begin to get involved in your duties as the pastor, you will soon come to know and identify the people of your congregation. You will begin to understand the eccentricities, complexities, and proclivities of those who are in the church and those you minister to over your career as a pastor. It will not take long to be able to identify the workers in the flock. You will see them running about frequently, working at their duties and you will notice their dedication and hard work getting things done. Many of these folks work quietly behind the scenes and usually do not announce their work. These people are dedicated to their position as a member of the church and a dedicated member of the body of Christ. They work hard and ask very little, if anything, in return. You are blessed beyond measure if you have a few of these folks in your congregation. I have enjoyed pastoring these people. One lady was in her seventies, yet, put in more hours behind the scenes than I did during the week. She was a really positive influence on my ministry at that church. I had to be careful mentioning something that needed to be done because she would try to take it on despite an already full schedule of her own. I have encountered a few more of these personalities and I have always said extra prayers for them because they continually give and give of themselves. God definitely has to be the source of their strength because even the Energizer Bunny runs down eventually!

You will become aware of who the complainers are too. These are the ones who are not happy with any decision that is made in the church and relish any opportunity that they get to corner you and tell you about it. They show up at all of the fellowship dinners and special programs but don't attend meetings and won't get involved in positive discussions and planning for the church. They tend to get upset quickly over any decision made by leadership. These folks love to complain, however, when invited to become a part of the process will quickly tell you that they *"don't want to get involved in church politics or be on any committee."* IF there is something that mysteriously pops out negatively in the community about your church, you may just have a pretty good idea where it originated. Tread softly though, there are some that will become known to you as whiners, but, that can be a false assumption! I have witnessed cases that these people were right about what they said and no one wanted to listen to them and they gave up trying and then became labeled by others as whiners.

There is another personality that you should be on the lookout for and I introduced you to them in the beginning of the chapter. Watch out for the *Delegator*! This is the one that loves to plan and create specific duties and details while expecting the rest of the congregants to carry them out with the proficiency of a well-trained military brigade.

This personality will create unwelcomed chaos in a church, and you can rest assured, that you are going to have people coming to you about the "*Delegator*" with no clue how to handle them. It may be a problem that is unexpectedly given over to you to handle, along with the comment that "*the last five pastors didn't have any luck with them either.*" BEWARE! This person will usually have a long association with the church and assume that through some right of age or tenure have attained the right to self-appoint themselves to their position. This is usually an issue more prevalent in the smaller congregations. If allowed, the "*Delegator*" will keep you endlessly hopping to their tune, and may often threaten to leave if confronted or questioned. They may be hoping that if they threaten to leave, they will be begged to remain. This person may even leave your church for a while if you don't take the bait, however, their curiosity of how the church may be getting along without them will eventually prove more than they can handle and they will show up one Sunday morning and act like they never left. Be aware of the infamous "*Delegator!*"

Once upon a time, in a land far far away, I was involved in a discussion with another pastor and we were discussing a new pastor that was coming into the area. The conversation that followed broke my heart. This church receiving the new pastor has one of those members that has benefited from familial and societal privilege. It can be problematic for the leaders in a congregation having to deal with a family member who expects to run the church because they give the most money. These members can be quick to point out how much money they give and how much they do for the church. It is easy to understand why the love of money was such an issue with Jesus. This personality can be very challenging for even a seasoned pastor. Sometimes these members are more worldly than spiritual so it can be difficult to handle them, even if you have a strong leadership team in place. While leaders may hesitate to be truthful with, or voting against these people, God has a unique way of working these situations out, if you trust God and have faith. Your leaders will gain strength from your faith. There are many wonderful families that have had great success in life and thank God for their success. They serve and give freely without a care of being recognized, so the one that tries to rule through the checkbook discredits the true faithful, fruitful, and charitable givers. There are wonderful families that are affluent and do everything they can to make their church a more welcoming and joyful house of worship.

These people are quick to give of their finances when necessary while allowing the leadership to do their jobs uninterrupted.

Another group you may face or be introduced to through learning the community are the ones that I call the bruised. These people were hurt by someone or something that occurred during their time in the church. These are further broken down into two groups. One group relates to those that were truly hurt and need to be comforted and receive restoration efforts. These folks are legitimate and present a wonderful opportunity for the pastor and leaders to be able to restore back into fellowship and back to a thriving relationship with their church family and with God.

The second group of bruised persons refers to the group that tells you they were bruised and then left and held onto their injury like it was a gold medal. No matter how hard you work to restore them they always revert back to how badly they were hurt. This group tends to become church pilgrims. They are on a search for something they cannot find. If you meet them and learn their history, there is a trail of bruising and hurt in their history that will prove exhausting. Sometimes the only reasonable answer is for you to just love them, pray for them, leave the door open and let God deal with them in his good time.

One more group that I want to share with you is the group I heard referred to as *"Pew Potatoes,"* These folks tend to think that after they got saved *if they got saved*, they just needed to sit on the pew for the rest of their life. They seem to be completely happy to bloom, die, and rot.... right there in the pews. These are the ones that Heaven and Earth cannot seem to move and they will prove to be a challenge for you to reach with all of your pastoral talents! You will hear a plethora of excuses as to why the *"Pew Potato"* cannot serve beyond keeping the seat warm. *"I am too old, I can't sing, I can't read scripture out loud, I can't testify,"* it always starts with *"I can't."* I am waiting to hear an original response such as *"my great grandmother and grandfather's sister's husband's cousin, once gave money to buy pews for the church and we are here to be sure we get our money's worth."* At least it would be an original response. I still try to motivate them as often as I can because I am waiting to be surprised when I least expect it. God has no limits and maybe one day they will realize that salvation is a gift, but also a task that involves their becoming involved too.

There may be a time that you will meet with some of these difficult personalities and find they are a member of your leadership teams. There are other difficult situations and scenarios that you may be required to deal with or lead your church through. How do you handle these difficult times? How do you have these difficult conversations? There may be times that you will sense a troubling spirit that has developed in the church. Do not kid yourself that this cannot happen because it can. It is how you handle it that will make the difference. If there comes a time that you have a significant issue that you will be required to address, call the members to a time of fervent prayer and fasting if necessary. Do not be tempted to handle an issue during the heat of a disagreement, but only after cool heads have had a chance to reflect and pray. I have a plan in place, which thankfully, I have never had to use. In the office of my first full-time pastorate, I had a crown of thorns and also some purple cloth. I had planned that if we had to go through something that was really important or particularly difficult, I would put the crown of thorns on one of the high backed pulpit chairs and hang the purple robe from it and encourage us all to take a moment and remember just exactly whose house of worship this really is and in whose name we are actually gathered. I pray that I will never have to implement and evaluate the success or failure of this plan.

The final item is not necessarily a problem but deserves mentioning simply because I have knowledge of many cases that were handled incorrectly. This group needs to be handled carefully, lovingly, and with much tact and care. This part is about our kids and we need to understand that kids are our next generation of leaders. It is easy to see that they are definitely in the minority, or at least in most of the church congregations that I have been involved. I have never heard a pastor comment that they have too many children in their church. Somewhere, we have lost a generation of kids and if you have the privilege of having a lot of kids in your church, get down on your knees and thank God for them and pray for their families!

Weekend sports, shopping, and all sorts of worldly activities have fought hard for the attention of society and the attention of church families, and sadly, have won many victories. Be happy if you have kids in the congregation. Do you have a good nursery? Do you have people that can take care of the kids during the worship service? Maybe you are a small church that doesn't have this ability. My philosophy is simple. Small kids need to be allowed to be their age. If I have parents with smaller kids, I make it a special point to go to them and let them know that it does not affect me if their child can't sit still or likes to wander in the church. Kids mimic what they see. As they grow in the church they will find their place so parents should be encouraged not to be embarrassed that their toddler cannot act like an adult. It is better they are in church than let at home! It just so happens that we have adults in the church that have difficulty acting like adults. If you don't believe me, watch what happens the next time your sermon goes over a few minutes! Be observant of how many times Brother Fumblefingers gets up and goes out of the sanctuary during service. Look in the pews after service and see how many fingernail clippings are on the back pew where Mrs. Flibbertygibbits sits, or at the bubble gum wrappers on the floor where Mr. Skippernoodle sits.

I remember a young family with a cute, rambunctious little girl. She was the boss in the house and everyone knew it. Mom and dad danced to her tune and dad was the one that usually was expected to handle her when the parental intervention was required. I remember on many occasions watching mom's face turn very red because the little girl couldn't sit still. She was a little girl and was not accustomed to being in church. Their fear was that she would make noise, and I think this kept them home despite my encouragement to come and let her get church experience. Cute little toddlers can steal the show in a heartbeat! Sometimes you just have to smile and thank God that you are living this experience. Twenty years from now that congregation will still remember that child and will also remember that the pastor was gentle and loving and not jealous that the child was being a child.

I remember a pastor that was getting ready to retire and was preaching one of his last sermons at his church. He had been their pastor for fifteen years. When he came there to pastor, there was a little fellow about three years old that crawled about the church during the service, and sometimes crawled right up to the pulpit and held on to the pastor's leg. The pastor would continue to preach with his new assistant close at hand. On this last service at retirement, the boy, now a grown young man, got up and went to the front of the church and sat at the pastor's feet as he began to preach. It took a bit for the pastor to realize what was happening, but those that remembered the many times they saw the little boy over the years, now saw the grown man now sitting around the pastor's feet and they were wiping teary eyes throughout the service. What a wonderful tribute to that pastor and what a memorable moment for those congregants!

I had one little fellow that was infamous for stealing the show on Wednesday night services. His mother and father worked long days but always brought their two children to services. Sometimes they arrived late but they always fed those children and settled them in for the service. One particular Wednesday, this little fella was stealing the show and came right up to the pulpit and extended his arms right in the middle of a rather fiery sermon. I reached down and picked him up and kept on preaching. He could only say a word or two, but, would occasionally point and grunt or try to imitate my mannerisms. It was a good evening. I look forward to seeing him as an adult.

So let us reflect on this chapter. There is a wide range of personalities in the church that you will be privileged to shepherd and some of them will make you earn your Pastor badge! You will encounter situations in which people will expect you to climb a mountain in the dark, and wrestle a bear, to complete a task that they are unwilling to cross the street on a sunny day to do themselves. You are certain to encounter issues with members that can lead to bigger problems if allowed to go unchecked. There are some problems that can be solved quickly with the right approach and attitude. Be wise and handle each occasion with prayer and wisdom. Don't let a hot temper give Satan a way to divide your church. Remember, you can do this! This chapter will most likely be one that you remember when you are writing your own future memoirs. Send me a copy, I would love to read about it!

Sometimes you reach the point that you have given it all you have to give and really feel in your heart that you have given your best effort but the results are just not there.

CHAPTER 14

The Next Chapter

The next chapter, the part that some will dread and for which others will yearn. The pathway of the pastor is a blank sheet of paper waiting for God to draw the lines. You may be at a church for one year, or for fifty years, but knowing when the voice of God is talking to you about moving to the next chapter of ministry is one of utmost importance. When you arrive at your church, you do not do so with the presence of thought that "this will do till God gives me something bigger or better." I also do not think that church boards call a pastor into a relationship with them by the same token either. "Well, this one isn't David Jeremiah, but, they will do till we can afford a smarter one." You arrive with the presence of thought that "I am going to serve here to the best of my ability and with the best of my talent and with all of my heart." Can I get an AMEN here?

I have had frank discussions with current board members about expectations of my performance as their pastor and expect them to hold me accountable. We have discussed expectations pertaining to my role as the shepherd as well as their role as the flock, and about how we can meet in the middle and work together. Although we have established roles for each of us, we are under the agreement that the presence and direction of the Holy Spirit working in our midst are more important than both of our roles. As long as we both live up to this agreement, things will work just fine. We know that God is always faithful.

So, how do you know that it is time to go? How do you know that it is time to be praying about whether or not God is ready to move you? One large denomination I am familiar with will take care of making that decision for you. They have established leadership that is responsible for relocating their pastors, however, both church and pastor do have some degree of input regarding their ability to stay or move. It is a lengthy process and I will not delve into it here.

The short answer is that I do not have the real answer as to when it is time to pack up and move on, however, I think that there are some gentle signals that will begin to be evidenced to you along the way and it will call your attention to reflection and prayer. As each new season of the year approaches, I look, listen, smell, and feel for the coming new change of season. I am always waiting for those first discernable signs of the changes I can identify. You should also be looking and feeling about the changes in your congregation. As you lead your people you will sense and feel what God is doing in your midst. Is your church growing? Is your church dying? Are the people getting along and working together? As you see or sense these things, you must examine yourself and be willing to ask the hard questions regarding, "Am I really doing what God is directing me to do, and am I doing it the way He tells me to do it?" Are the church members and board supporting your efforts to lead, and are they meeting you in the middle?

Remember in the first chapters where I talked about following another pastor? As the new pastor, did you have to help heal any wounds that the congregation may have had before you arrived? If there were wounds that did not heal, they only worsened, and may now be negatively affecting the health of your current ministry. Maybe the beginning of your pastoral duties at that church started out with a struggle. You realize you just don't seem to be connecting with the people like you thought you should. Did they have a pastor that had been with them for a long time or one that led them through some really tough times? Were they someone that the congregation really adored and respected? Have you allowed them the opportunity to grieve that loss and come to terms with their loss of that pastor? If you have not realized it and helped them through the healing process, they have not been able to properly connect with you because of those previous feelings of loss. This is especially difficult if the previous pastor died while serving them. The other side of that coin is that the previous pastor went through the congregation like the proverbial tornado through the trailer park, wreaking havoc and scattering the sheep. Do not be fooled, there are plenty of those out there, and one or two may even read this book.

What is happening in your congregation? Are they engaging with you and with each other, and with the community? Are they serving? Are they generous with their giving? Are you seeing souls added to the kingdom of God? Are you baptizing people and adding new members to the body of Christ? If these answers are NO, what is the reason? When I pastored multiple churches, one of the many reports that I was responsible to submit each year, dealt with these types of questions. When you look back over the past five years of church history and data and see that a church has not listed anyone being saved or added members, but steadily lost members, this is a humongous red flag that this church is potentially dying and in dire need of a rapid intervention!

If the church has lost members regularly since your arrival that should be a quick red flag that is calling for your attention. Did you arrive to learn the previous pastor of your church left to go and pastor a church up the road from you and then courted away your members? That happens frequently in small communities. Pastors will get upset and leave and go to another church and then try to convince your members that they need to come and follow them in their new ministry. Another reason may be that someone in the church decided that they could pastor better than the current shepherd and left to start their own ministry. They did not want to follow the proper and approve paths to ministry because *"me and Jesus got our own thing going,"* so they left and soon came courting your members because they needed the money to stay afloat and also wanted to increase their numbers and thumb their nose at the previous church; which, caused such an issue that it may have led to the previous pastor becoming disheartened enough to leave.

Have you changed some things in the church that was actually working because you did not like them, or felt it could be done differently? Does the administration regularly refuse to work with you on a proposed change, or changes, that you felt was truly in the best interest of the church?

Does your leadership meetings resemble a three-ring circus complete with monkeys? Where I am headed with this is to ask you if the problem in the church preventing the growth is a pastoral issue, an administrative issue, or a spiritual issue. If these issues cannot be addressed and overcame, this is a good sign that the problem may need to be resolved with an administrative change or a pastoral change.

Sometimes you reach the point that you have given it all you have to give and really feel in your heart that you have given your best effort but the results are just not there. You may love the people and the people may love you, but the church is just not doing well. This is definitely a time for discernment and prayer. I suggest inviting the leadership and the members to pray together with you and ask for God to reveal the way. Your first thought might be that you failed, but try to hold off on thinking this way as this may also be God's way of getting your attention. God may have placed you where you are for a season and for a reason, and now that season may be over.

Maybe you get called into an impromptu administrative meeting that you were not aware was being called. You are now the guest of honor, and you are being informed that it is a really good time for you to leave and the church wants to call a new pastor. That one kind of removes all the guesswork for you. It may also be an answered prayer if there was a toxic atmosphere that you had been serving under. It is possible that you have known for some time that things were not working and you were not being successful in your efforts to improve them. Again, this does not represent failure. Maybe you were not seeing the signs or hearing the whispers of God's Spirit. Sometimes, God is dealing with the church people and it has nothing to do with your leadership ability or your abilities as a pastor. Sadly, some churches have a history of dealing dirty and they will answer to God for their behavior.

In all honesty, I believe that it boils down to what you are feeling inside as you follow the guidance of the Holy Spirit. He may choose to lead you to another church, lead you across denominational lines, lead you across the country, or even lead you around the world! If you are dedicated and following the voice and direction of God, you will know when it is the right time to make a move, and no committee or board can argue otherwise. I would only advise you to be sure that if you are experiencing a restlessness of your spirit, be sure to confirm it is God speaking to you and not you listening to your own flesh. That will spell trouble. If it is God leading you, the evidence will be there, and the doors will open in their due season as God leads you along.

Remember that pastoral ministry is like the song, "One day at a time sweet Jesus." Do not be concerned about whether you will learn it all, you will not even come close. Just be faithful and trust God!

Conclusion

That's a Wrap Folks!

Oh my! Are we at the end already? It has been almost a year since I began this book. I have been finishing my pastoral studies and getting settled in with our new church family, so the book had to wait a bit longer but that is perfectly fine. I am moving into my sixth year in pastoral ministry and wanted to put pen to paper before I forgot what a lot of those first experiences were like and how they affected me. As I have gone back and proofread a bit, I realize that I have not scratched the surface in the least, but wanted to put something in writing that was manageable for you as the new pastor.

Anyhow, let us begin to wrap up this journey and bring the train into the station! You will notice that I did not specifically address administrative issues in this book. Your administration abilities are going to grow as you gain experience. As you go forward there will be people that are going to be there to help you along the way. Depending on what type of church you serve, you will have outlines for how administrative policies and issues will be expected to be handled. Do not worry too much, you will be one that either has good administrative skills or has administrative skills that need improving. You may need to take a class here and there or solicit help when and where you can to shore up your abilities. Remember, God does not always call the equipped! Learn what your church or denomination expects and start getting involved in learning where the church stands in relation to those expectations.

I will offer one small piece of advice, well alright, it is a huge one. Be extremely diligent and careful pertaining to church finances. You do not want to personally handle money in the church nor do you want your spouse handling the money. Knowing all of the aspects of income and expenditures of your church is important but personally handling the money is a huge no-no for the pastor! You can imagine that if there are questions over finances or accusations of misappropriation where the fingers are going to point. Be sure you cover your bases and keep good records and you should be ok. Consider obtaining your own malpractice insurance as these days, someone could sue you for sneezing in the wrong direction.

Remember that pastoral ministry is like the song, "One day at a time sweet Jesus." Do not be concerned about whether you will learn it all, you will not even come close. Just be faithful and trust God! When you reach your first year anniversary, celebrate it with your spouse! I think that it is a huge milestone for you to achieve and you should really take some time to reflect on that journey and realize how far you have come. Although I personally stink at this, consider keeping a journal to write down some specific milestones as you go along. Write down your first experiences with dates and times so you can go back later and see how far God has brought you.

In conclusion, I have obviously fallen way short of re-inventing the wheel, but, I hope I have given you some things to think about, and have offered you some insight regarding some of the curve balls that will be thrown at you, and the pitfalls that may await you. I hope that if you find yourself facing one of these areas that you will be better equipped to handle it with tact and professionalism. I hope that as you have journeyed this far along with me, you are able to say it was worth the effort you expended and the few dollars you spent to be able to share in this information. Who knows, you may even be moved to share this book with another pastor along the way, or give a new pastor their own copy as a gift. This is not about the money. My prayer is that this will be blessed by God and become a tool that really and truly helps another pastor have a better picture of what lies ahead as they embark on a life long journey in the service of our Lord and Savior, Jesus Christ. Maybe you will embrace the desire to help the new pastors you will meet along the way as well.

May God bless you and keep you all the days of your life and may your days in ministry be long and fruitful. Take my prayers and best wishes with you as you surge forth in ministry to declare Jesus Christ to the world. Amen.

Matthew 28 King James Version

19 Go ye therefore, and teach all nations, baptizing them in the name of the Father, and of the Son, and of the Holy Ghost:

20 Teaching them to observe all things whatsoever I have commanded you: and, lo, I am with you always, even unto the end of the world. Amen.

About the Author

Robby Shorter resides in southern West Virginia and serves as the lead pastor of Pineville Church of the Nazarene. Prior to coming to Pineville and the Church of the Nazarene family, he had served as pastor to six churches in the WV Conference of the UMC.

Robby has an Associate's Degree in Nursing from Bluefield State College. He holds a District Ministers License in the WV South District of the Church of the Nazarene, and is actively pursuing ordination as an Elder, having recently finished his required studies that were begun at the Course of Study School of Ohio, and completed at the WV South District Church of the Nazarene School of Ministry.

In his secular career, Robby has worked extensively in the healthcare system and developed a complex resume, one requiring many different classes and certifications. He began working in the EMS field in 1983 and graduated from the Nursing Program in 1997. His resume involves the areas of expertise including ambulances, medical command telecommunications, hospital, medical helicopter, EMS telecommunication, 911 telecommunication, and volunteer firefighter.

Robby grew up beside the WV Turnpike watching and loving tractor trailers. He has enjoyed extensive travel in forty-four of the lower forty-eight states as a professional tractor trailer driver. He was privileged to teach for a short time, at a professional driver training school. This was the very same school that had trained him 25 years earlier.

Robby and his wife Debbie have been married since 1987 and they have one son, Josh.

Printed in the United States
By Bookmasters